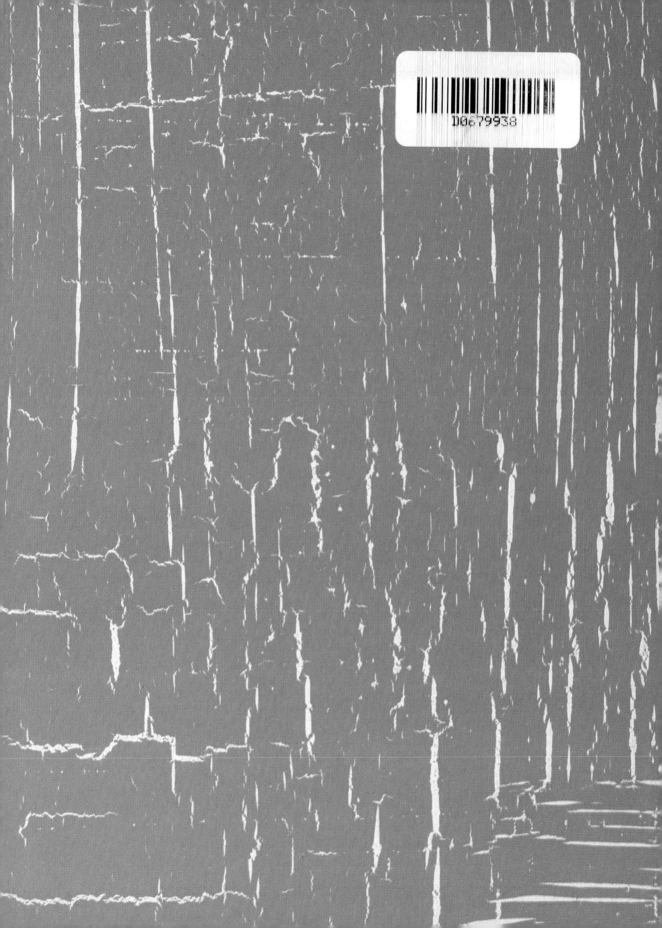

FANTASY FINISHES

PAINT TECHNIQUES FOR INTERIORS
FURNITURE AND OBJECTS

DAVIES
·
KEELING
·
TROWBRIDGE

WITH JOHN WAINWRIGHT

Macdonald Orbis

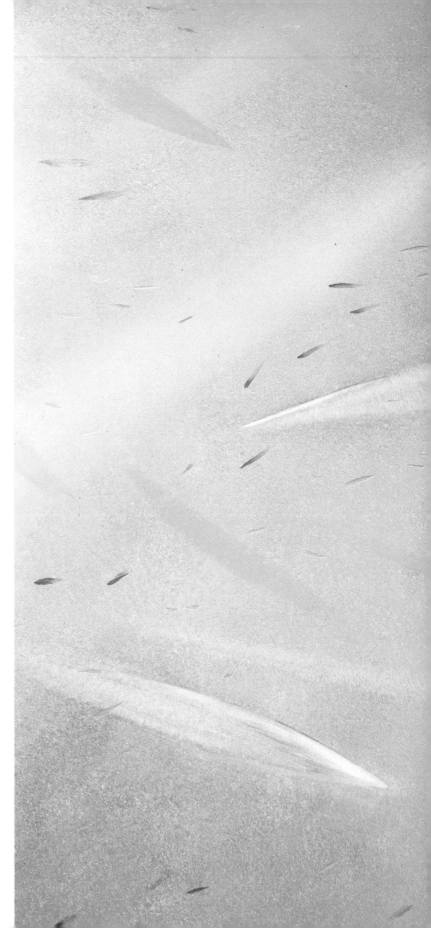

A *Macdonald Orbis* BOOK

ⓒ Macdonald Orbis 1989

First Published in Great Britain in 1989 by
Macdonald & Co (Publishers) Ltd
London & Sydney

A member of Maxwell Pergamon Publishing
Corporation plc

British Library Cataloguing in Publication Data
Wainwright, John
Fantasy Finishes
1. Residences. Interior Design — Amateurs' manuals
1. Title
747

ISBN 0-356-17601-0

Filmset by Jahweh Associates
Printed and bound in Italy by Graphicom

Senior Commissioning Editor: Judith More
Senior Art Editor: Clive Hayball
Editor: Phil Wilkinson
Designer: David Riley
Photographers: Dave King, Jerry Tubby, Susannah
Price
Picture researcher: Cathy Lockley

Macdonald & Co (Publishers) Ltd
Headway House
66-73 Shoe Lane
London EC4P 4AP

contents

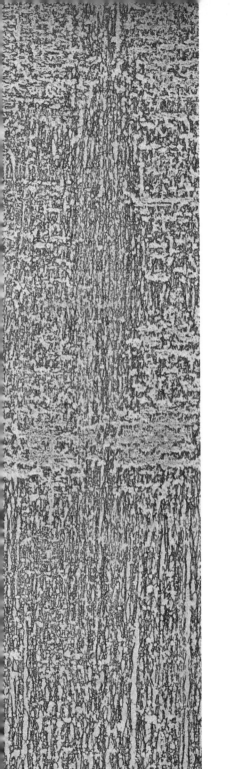

introduction

THE DESIRE TO EMBELLISH OUR SURROUNDINGS
with pattern and colour, to create a
visually pleasing environment that both mirrors
and projects our personality and sense of taste, is
a basic human characteristic that can be traced
back to the cave paintings of our primitive
ancestors. Fortunately, paint has long since
superseded charcoal and blood as the primary
medium for decoration. And, in addition to better
materials, the intervening years have also
provided us with a wealth of decorative
techniques and ideas, many of which have been
adapted from fine art ▶

For centuries artists and decorative painters have exploited these (broken colour) techniques – such as ragging, sponging, stippling and dragging – in combination with the various properties of colour, paints and translucent tinted glazes, to both please and trick the eye. They have used them to simulate the appearance of diverse, often expensive, materials such as marble (Marbling), wood (Woodgraining), precious stones and metal, on commonplace surfaces such as canvas and plaster; as well as employing them to visually adjust the architectural proportions of rooms and buildings, enhance furniture and artefacts and, in combination with simple perspective and shading, to give a three-dimensional quality to otherwise flat, two-dimensional surfaces and objects.

In this book we draw on this long tradition to present a variety of decorative finishes, based on quite simple broken colour techniques, which can be used to enhance all manner of surfaces around your home. Some of the finishes, such as Verdigris, Plaster, Stone Block, Watered Silk or Porphyry (see pages 96-107 and 120-1), are, as their names imply, simulations of organic and man-made materials and objects. Others, like Blazer (see pages 116-7), Nebula (see pages 122-3), Antiquing (see pages 108-9) and Crackle (see pages 108-11), depict a variety of natural phenomena and processes. While Tiffany (see pages 118-9) and Two-Colour Distressing (see pages 112-3)

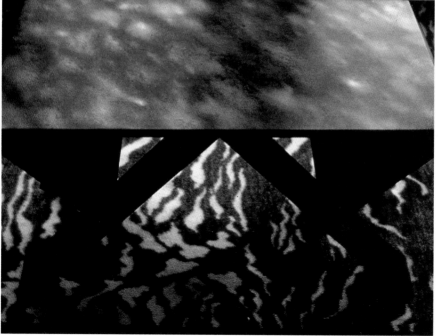

Above: *Brown eggshell and silver metallic glazes have been combined in a dramatic Blazer effect (see pages 116-7) to embellish this recessed wall panel. Bold Fantasy Finishes such as this are often most effective if restricted to panel areas, rather than taken over an entire wall.*

Left: *Don't feel that you have to slavishly copy the colours shown in our simulations – here iridescent blue and pink glazes were used for an 'unnatural' Beast finish (see pages 120-1) to decorate the top of this coffee table, and echo the Zebra skin pattern of the woven rug.*

Left: *You can transform all manner of objects with a Fantasy Finish. Originally intended for displaying garden shrubs, this inexpensive terracotta wall vase has become a stylish lacquered 'bronze' uplighter at the hands of designer Jon Lys Turner. Small patches of verdigris have also been simulated, to 'weather' and 'age' the finish (for technique, see Metal Patina – Verdigris, pages 96-7).*

Above: *Featureless homes can be given character with a suitable Fantasy Finish. Here routed M.D.F. (medium density fibreboard) panelling has been decorated with a blue Metal Patina effect (see pages 96-7). The eggshell and metallic glazes used in the finish co-ordinate with the carpet and cast a diffused reflection of the light, which enhances the sense of space.*

simply employ subtle combinations of colour and pattern to create an abstract decorative effect.

The first part of the book, which is intended to be inspirational, looks at how these finishes can be incorporated into decorative schemes in the various rooms around the house – providing an opportunity to view and assess them, as it were, *in situ*. The book's second part gives advice on how to prepare a wide range of surfaces around the home to take a Fantasy Finish; details the paints, glazes and equipment you will need and outlines a method for mixing your own glazes; provides an introduction to some of the properties of colours – giving advice on how to use them to create a variety of decorative effects; explains methods for working over large areas; and finally, shows you, in an illustrated step-by-step sequence, how to reproduce the finishes themselves.

At first you will probably wish to make a faithful copy of any finish as it is demonstrated in the illustrated step-by-step sequence. However, having gained in experience and confidence, you are encouraged to make colour and compositional adjustments to suit your own decorative requirements. Indeed, some suggested alternatives are shown at the end of the step-by-step instructions, and many of the pictures in the first half of the book display a number of decorative effects that are either modifications of the basic finishes, or are created by combining techniques drawn from more than one finish. For example, a bronze-gold Metal Patina effect can be created from the first four steps of the Verdigris finish, while techniques taken from Watered Silk and Antiquing can be combined to create a 'Patine' finish, and elements of Two-Colour Distressing can be absorbed into the Plaster finish.

Moreover, it is important to remember that successful results do not necessarily depend on authentic replication of any particular subject or phenomena. On the contrary, many of the finishes, notably Lapis Lazuli, Porphyry and Verdigris, are both striking and effective simply because they capture the essential characteristics, if you like, the essence, of the subject – it is this more than anything else you should strive for when creating Fantasy Finishes.

Opposite left: *The warm, mellow tones of mahogany joinery have been cleverly combined with a blue and red Two-Colour Distressed finish on a yellow base (see pages 112-3), to offset the cool cast of the bathroom fittings.*

Left: *The red and yellow glazes work particularly well with mahogany, as they are all hues to be found in the wood itself.*
Below: *There is a pleasing textural contrast between the soft wall finish and the hard chrome and enamel.*

chapter one

halls, stairways and landings

BY VIRTUE OF THEIR LOCATION, ENTRANCE
halls provide visitors with their first impressions
of the inside of a home, and adjacent corridors,
stairways and landings establish a visual link
between the various rooms that lead off them. In
so doing, the appearance of these all too often
neglected areas can make a significant
contribution to the style and atmosphere of any
domestic interior, and they should be decorated
accordingly.

When deciding upon a decorative scheme for an entrance hall and stairway it is important to make an initial assessment of the architectural aspects and features of the area, and decide which ones you want to emphasise, or highlight, and which you would like to disguise.

For example, small, narrow, poorly-lit hallways can provide a cramped, unwelcoming entrance to a home – an unwanted effect that may be exaggerated by the use of dark, strongly contrasting colours in the decor. However, by applying a Fantasy Finish such as Plaster effect (see pages 104-5), Two-Colour Distressing (see pages 112-3) or Tiffany (see pages 118-9) in light colours, carrying it over the walls, mouldings, and possibly the doors as well, you will establish a feeling

of continuity, make surfaces and features 'recede', and thereby increase the sense of space.

Indeed, the glazes used can be adjusted as necessary to make these finishes subtly lighter or darker at different points along a surface – a useful option when decorating a long corridor or stairway that is gloomier at one end than the other. Similarly, a high ceiling that exaggerates the narrowness of a hall or landing, and makes the area feel 'colder' than it really is, can be visually lowered, either by painting it in a darker shade than the walls below, or by carrying over the Fantasy Finish from the walls. On the other hand, a low ceiling can be visually raised by painting it in a lighter tint than the surfaces below it – an effect that is enhanced by gradually lightening the finish on the walls as it approaches the ceiling.

However, even in confined areas where subtle finishes and pale colours are called for to increase the sense of space, don't feel restricted to using a single finish. It is possible to feature particular fixtures and fittings without making the area appear cluttered. For example, a pale Stone Block finish (see pages 100-1) on the walls can be offset to good effect by a run of doors, architrave, dado rail and skirting flat painted in a

Below: *Picking up colours in the carpet, the fluted spindles of this ornate stair rail have been given a bronze Verdigris finish (see pages 96-7). The dark mahogany bannister rail and risers provide a stylish contrast that emphasises the elegant proportions of the staircase.*

Right: *To create this wall finish turquoise and green glazes were brushed and wiped out in all directions over a yellow ground coat, in a boldly composed adaptation of the Plaster effect (see pages 104-5). The yellow basecoat ghosting through the finish co-ordinates with the mellow patina of the walnut veneered chiffonier and mirror, and the stained pine doors and architrave, while echoing the warm tones of the exposed brickwork and tiled floor.*

Above: *In this hallway, the painter has created a striking Stone Block finish (see pages 100-1) on the walls above dado height. Additional shading has been employed to emphasise the mortar lines, and establish an impressive three-dimensional quality. Atmospheric lighting enhances this effect. Below this, a lightly sponged paler finish has been augmented with trompe l'oeil panelling (see pages 104-5).*

Left: *Michael Synder carried a Stone Block effect (see pages 100-1) around the walls of this stairwell, providing an historically appropriate backdrop to the 'medieval' tapestries. The sand-coloured glazes in the finish, and the rich mellow patina of the light oak staircase, are effectively combined with an abundance of artificial light to create a bright, warm and spacious interior – not often the case in a stairwell.*

slightly darker tone, or by the spindles of the staircase picked out in a bronze/copper Metal Patina effect (see pages 96-7).

While picking out features in small hallways usually requires a restrained use of colour and pattern if you are to avoid closing down the space, larger entrances and stairways offer greater scope for employing darker, warmer colours and bolder compositions. For example, a Beast (see pages 120-1) or Blazer effect (see pages 116-7) carried over the walls in the entrance hall and up the stairs from landing to landing, will invariably make a dramatic impact, while maintaining a sense of continuity. Similarly, a pastiche Stone Block finish executed in vibrant, saturated colours – yellows, for example – and offset by natural wood or Metal Patina doors and skirtings will prove equally striking. In both examples the translucency of the glazes used and the method of application create a sense of depth in the surface that ensures the strident colours don't become overbearing.

However, larger areas can be decorated just as impressively with the paler, more subtle finishes suggested for smaller halls. Thus the Plaster effect (see pages 104-5) can be carried successfully over ceilings and walls; but in this case, the scale of the surfaces may allow you to superimpose the finish over stencilled motifs – the latter ghosting through the translucent glazes like aged frescoes – or to combine it with *trompe l'oeil* features such as recessed panelling (see pages 104-5), Porphyry pillars or Stone Block archways. In other words, when decorating larger, architecturally 'bland' areas, there is often a case for using paints and glazes to create additional features, as well as highlighting those that are already there.

Above left: *In this fine example of Stone Blocking (see pages 100-1), the painter has made subtle colour and compositional changes from block to block, adding to the realism of the effect, as such variations are usually found in the natural stone. Carrying the finish over buttresses, archways and other features helps to emphasise the architectural proportions of the room – provided the blocks are 'cut' realistically.*

Left: *An exotic Beast effect (see pages 120-1) has been used to decorate the walls of this entrance hall and stairwell. The combination of a white ceiling, off-white stair carpet and floor tiles, and generous lighting provides a bright, neutral contrast to the warm yellows, reds and browns of the Beast finish, and ensures its impact, on such a scale, is flamboyant and dramatic rather than dark and overbearing.*

Left: *On the walls and columns of this grand entrance area a Plaster finish (see pages 104-5) has been cleverly combined with classical motifs and murals to simulate the appearance of aged and weathered frescoes.*

Right: *A Plaster effect (see pages 104-5) has been used to decorate the side walls and moulded coving of this imposing hallway. The understated paint finish makes an harmonious contrast to the gold metallic motif wallpaper on the facing walls and ceiling, and the subtle off-white marbling around the skirting, and thus helps to define the elegant architectural proportions of the room.*

But regardless of the size and scale of the hall and stairway, when choosing a decorative scheme you should take into account how your proposed finish will link with the rooms that lead off. This is obviously important where a corridor leads straight into a room via an open archway – in which case the colour and composition of the finishes on either side of the arch should either be the same, or work harmoniously together. Thus, a Plaster effect (see pages 104-5) would successfully run into Two-Colour Distressing (see pages 112-3), provided the latter was executed in colours of a similar hue and tone, but the strident diagonal accent and the brown, red and black hues of Beast (see pages 120-1) might sit uncomfortably next to the swirling blues of Lapis Lazuli (see pages 98-9).

Relating the colours and finishes of adjacent areas to each other is less of a problem if they are separated by a closed door. However, when the door is open a visual link is established – the room can be seen from the hallway, and *vice versa*; and any finish on the hall side of the door itself temporarily becomes part of the decorative scheme in the room.

Yet the extent to which your choice of a decorative scheme for the hallway is determined by the finishes employed in adjacent rooms ultimately depends on the type of interior you wish to create. On the one hand you might want a co-ordinated decorative scheme throughout your entire home, in which the fantasy colours and compositions of individual rooms should subtly merge into each other via the hallway, stairs and landings. On the other, you may envisage your home as a collection of strongly contrasting areas, each with its own mutually exclusive style and atmosphere. Both approaches can be equally successful, provided you avoid putting obviously discordant or clashing colours and finishes in close proximity to one another.

chapter two

living rooms

LIVING ROOMS COME IN A NUMBER OF GUISES:
formal reception areas reserved for special
occasions and entertaining guests; communal
family rooms in which to relax, listen to music,
watch television and eat informal meals; and
rooms which, often out of necessity, must
accommodate all the above functions, and more
. . . such as serving, in part, as a study-cum-
library, or putting up friends overnight on a
sofabed. Obviously the use to which your living
room is put should play some part in the choice of a
decorative scheme.

Living rooms which play host to all manner of communal or family activities, are usually crowded with numerous pieces of furniture, soft furnishings, electrical appliances, books, magazines and personal possessions etc. In these circumstances, it is important to choose a decorative scheme which doesn't add to any sense of clutter or chaos – unless, of course, this is a style you wish to cultivate!

A good finish to choose is Two-Colour Distressing (see pages 112-3), which could be executed in soft, muted pastel colours (perhaps matched to hues found in the carpet or curtains) and lightened with a highly translucent milky-white glaze, and carried around the walls and over any fitted bookcases or shelving. This will provide an elegant but unobtrusive background to the hive of human activity. Moreover, by decorating a throw or cushions for the sofa, using the same finish – or one such as Porphyry (see pages 102-3) or Aquarium (see pages 114-5) executed in the same soft, pastel colours – you will bring an element of co-ordination, and therefore some sense of cohesion, to the otherwise disparate elements in the room.

Obviously in a small room there is a good argument for incorporating features such as bookcases, doors, architrave, dado rails and skirting boards into the finish on the surrounding walls. In other words, 'losing' them in the background, thereby allowing the eye to move relatively uninterrupted around the perimeter of the

Right: *The walls of this living room have been painted by Michael Snyder with a subtle Two-Colour Distressed finish (see pages 112-3). The mottled yellow glazes, enhanced by soft uplighting, help to create a bright, warm and cosy atmosphere. Indeed, the gentle gradations of colour and the lightly scrubbed texture of a Two-Colour Distressed finish will usually, as here, provide a suitably understated backdrop to an eclectic display of furniture, pictures and other decorative objects.*

Right: *In this detail of the room shown opposite, the yellow Two-Colour Distressed walls provide a pleasantly contrasting backdrop to the Metal Patina effect (see pages 96-7) on top of a built-in cupboard. The colours in, and to some extent the composition of, the finish are taken from the yellow and gold decorative biscuit tin, while a steel blue and gray (real) metal vase provides an appropriate contrast.*

room – an effect which visually increases the overall sense of space.

On the other hand, picking out features in a different finish to the one used on the walls or ceiling – such as linking up the doors, architrave, dado and skirting in a sponged or wiped, pale yellow finish and setting them against a Plaster effect (see pages 104-5) on the walls – will help to define the architectural proportions and scale of the room – which, of course, may not be desirable in a small area. Moreover, the stronger the colour and compositional contrast between the picked-out feature and the background surface, the more this effect will be accentuated.

But this is not to say that strong, saturated colours and strident compositions should never be used in anything other than large, spacious rooms; far from it. Indeed, even in relatively small living areas there is considerable scope for employing dramatic finishes,

Below and right: *The walls of this large drawing room have been decorated with a Verdigris Metal Patina finish (for technique see pages 96-7). The green eggshell and bronze-gold metallic glazes combine to cast a soft, fragmented sheen that reflects both natural and artificial light – an effect that contributes to the sense of space in this room, and complements the mellow patina of the stained and polished wooden fire surround, bookcase, double doors and flooring.*

Above: *The translucent pale green glazes normally applied at the end of the Verdigris finish (see pages 96-7) have in this instance only been brushed out over the walls, thereby leaving a contrasting, darker finish on the panel mouldings and skirting board. This simple omission adds visual interest to large expanses of wall, and helps to define the architectural qualities of a room.*

such as Metal Patina (see pages 96-7), Blazer (see pages 116-7) and Beast (see pages 120-1). However, they must be used with discretion, and in most cases are better confined to relatively small surface areas.

For example, a quite ordinary plaster or wooden fire surround, when embellished with a striking red and black Blazer effect (see pages 116-7), or a dark, intense Porphyry finish (see pages 102-3), will provide a compelling focal point in an otherwise subdued decorative scheme. Moreover, by taking the effect over its entire surface, and making no concession in the use of colour and composition to the structure of the surround, you can break down and disguise ugly or indifferent form and line while giving 'presence' to the object as a whole — a technique that can be usefully employed over almost any surface. Thus a commonplace, and rather 'boxy', hi-fi unit and pair of speakers, decorated in a scaled-down and gloss-varnished Nebula effect (see pages 122-3), can be given a monumental solidity, softness of line and depth of finish that belies their original cost and quality of construction.

As with fire surrounds, small alcoves and niches can be picked out using quite striking finishes, which would appear overstated if applied over larger areas in a smallish room. Thus a vibrant, electric blue Watered Silk effect (see pages 106-7), or a bronze or copper-

Left: *The two-tone blue distressed finish on the wall panelling in this ornate interior can be simulated by following the first five steps of the Watered Silk technique (see pages 106-7).*

Above: *In this large drawing room a nicely understated Stone Block finish (see pages 100-1) picks up a colour in the sofa fabric and echoes the geometric pattern of the plain white dado panelling.*

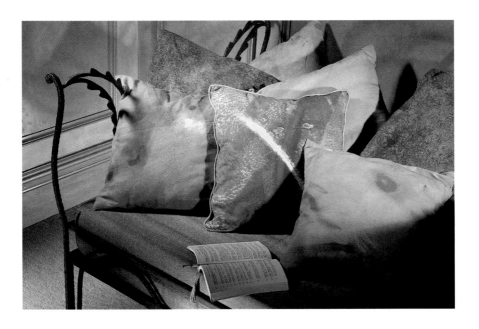

Below: *The pale yellow and sand Two-Colour Distressing on the walls (see pages 112-3) provides a warm background for the prints and decorative objects.*
Left: *Soft furnishings can be given a Fantasy Finish. Here, cushions have been painted in Beast (see pages 120-1), Porphyry (see pages 102-3), and Aquarium (see pages 114-5) finishes.*
Right: *The yellow and sand colours of the walls and flooring are picked up in the greeny-brown Plaster effect on the ceiling (see pages 104-5).*

Left: *In this period panelled room the chimney breast and fitted bookcases in the alcoves on either side of it have been given a subtly distressed, or 'aged', finish known as 'Patine', which can be produced by adapting the Watered Silk and Antiquing techniques (see caption below).*

Right: *A slightly darker version of the 'Patine' has been applied to the walls to co-ordinate with the window shutters and joinery elsewhere in the room.*

Above: *This detail reveals fine threads of colour running through the finish, which can be achieved by dragging a lighter glaze over a darker one, using the dragging technique described in Watered Silk (see pages 106-7), then rubbing it back (see Antiquing, pages 108-9).*

coloured beaten Metal Patina finish (see pages 96-7), might be confined to a pair of small wall niches, and offset by a subtle, understated pale gray or yellow Porphyry finish (see pages 102-3) taken over the surrounding walls.

Obviously in a relatively large, spacious living room, where the inhabitants and their possessions make less demand on both the actual and perceived sense of space, stronger darker colours, bold compositions and vivid contrasts can be used on a grander scale. However, it is just as important to combine different finishes with discretion, and to avoid discordant or clashing colours and compositions – even in the most theatrical of decorative schemes.

Thus in a neo-Gothic setting, in which Antiqued Stone Block walls (see pages 100-1 and 108-9), are combined with aged and torn Beast (see pages 120-1) and Watered Silk (see pages 106-7) painted floorcloths and 'tapestries', it would be appropriate to use a Verdigris finish (see pages 96-7) on the doors, to simulate an authentic weathered bronze effect. Whereas, in such a room a vivid, light blue Aquarium finish (see pages 114-5) on the woodwork would seem somewhat incongrous and clash with the rest of the decor.

Of course, many homes have relatively large reception areas as a result of knocking previously separate living and dining rooms into one, the two now being joined by an open archway, or less commonly, pairs of folding doors. While the architectural features are almost always similar in both areas, they are often to some extent divided by function, and therefore different types of furniture. For example, one half might contain upholstered seating, a television and hi-fi; while the other, a desk, bookshelves, a small table and occasional chairs. In these circumstances you have two options: you can either further define the room into two separate areas by choosing distinct, but compatible, decorative schemes for each 'half', or you can take the alternative route of employing one scheme throughout in order to unify them. If you opt for separate schemes you could either employ different finishes executed in the same colours – for example soft pinky-blue Watered Silk and Tiffany finishes – or use the same finish in each half, but in different colours (perhaps with a cooler colour at the sunnier end and a warmer one in the colder half).

Finally, spacious rooms often display large, visually bland surfaces; notably, long expanses of bare wall. But just as decorative paint finishes can be used to minimise the impact of elaborate architectural features in small rooms, so they can be used to create them in larger ones. Thus, for example, *trompe l'oeil* recessed panelling (see pages 104-5), buttresses and fluted columns can be convincingly 'built into' Plaster, Porphyry or Stone Block walls, and successfully combined with either stencilled motifs or hand-painted murals. This is particularly effective in feature-less modern rooms. Of course, the emphasis placed on producing correct scale and proportion when creating these images will be largely determined by whether you are concerned to create an 'authentic' or a fantasy finish.

Above left and opposite: *The decorative finish in this well-furnished living room was inspired by the sofa fabric. A rich red glaze was applied over the walls and doors, and then gold metallic paint was wiped on top of this in the panelling and below dado height, to simulate a contrasting Metal Patina effect (see pages 96-7). Both the colours and the texture of the distressed finish provide a suitably opulent backdrop for the gilt-framed pictures and antique furniture, and complement the ornately carved rail around the gallery above. The high ceiling, large windows and abundance of natural light (the latter softly reflected by the metallic paint) ensure the dark colours don't close down the sense of space.*

chapter three

kitchens and dining rooms

BY VIRTUE OF THEIR FUNCTION, KITCHENS
have always been at the heart of the home. And
while slaving over a hot stove or the sink has been
tempered by the advent of the microwave and
dishwasher, a considerable amount of time is still
spent in this room – even more so when it is
sufficiently large to double-up as a dining area,
and therefore a place in which to entertain guests.
In these circumstances, the aesthetics of the
design are just as important as the ergonomics of
the layout – a principle equally applicable when
choosing a scheme for a separate dining room.

Most modern fitted kitchens are designed around mass-produced storage units and appliances which, while making for an efficient, hygienic and streamlined working environment, unfortunately tend to give the room an air of anonymous uniformity. Even very expensive, hand-built kitchen units will often not appear as unique as perhaps they ought to. However, by employing decorative paint finishes to either subtly co-ordinate with, or totally transform, the appearance of the existing layout, you will be able to put the stamp of originality on your own kitchen.

If the kitchen unit doors are faced either with a drab melamine coating, or a cheap and rather boring wood veneer, they could be thoroughly rubbed down, primed, undercoated, eggshelled (see *Preparation of surfaces*, with special reference to Melamine, page 73) and finally painted with a Fantasy Finish. The colours and composition you choose will be partly determined by the size of the room, the amount of natural and artificial light, and whether or not they have to co-ordinate with existing furniture, window blinds, flooring and an adjacent dining area etc . . .

Thus, in a large, spacious kitchen or kitchen/diner, the units could be successfully embellished with a bold, red and black Blazer finish (see pages 116-7), or a copper Metal Patina effect (see pages 96-7), and offset by a light gray Porphyry (see pages 102-3) taken over the walls, and possibly onto any blinds or curtains at the windows. The ceiling could be lightly sponged in a matching off-white or soft pastel colour.

Clearly the Metal Patina and Blazer finishes might prove overbearing on fitted units in a smaller, darker setting. In which case, a light Tiffany (see pages 118-9) or Aquarium (see pages 114-5) effect would be more suitable – one or more of the pale colours perhaps being sponged or stippled over the other surfaces to create a feeling of cohesion, and thereby increase the sense of space.

Of course many fitted kitchen units are of pleasing proportions, and faced with elegant, attractive and expensive veneers, to paint over which would be tantamount to vandalism. However, they can be offset to good effect by running a subtle finish such as Two-Colour Distressing (see pages 112-3), Plaster (see pages 104-5) or Porphyry (see pages 102-3), over the walls and along the splashback between the floor and wall units. The colours you use should work harmoniously, rather than compete, with the units. And they can be mixed to make the room appear either warmer or cooler, as necessary. Thus, two tones of vibrant yellow used in a Two-Colour Distressed finish would work well with mahogany units, as might a pale green Porphyry effect. But the latter would create a cooler,

Above: *Bare walls above dado height were clear gloss-varnished (see page 89) to enhance the subtle configuration of colours in the old plaster.*
Below: *Michael Synder blended in sections of new plaster using a combination of the Plaster (see pages 104-5) and Two-Colour Distressing (see pages 112-3). Shelving was Antiqued (see pages 108-9).*
Right: *Below dado height, the walls and cupboards were given a distressed Verdigris finish (see pages 96-7).*

Left: *The vibrant yellow, Two-Colour Distressed finish (see pages 112-3) on the walls of this dining area complement the stained and varnished pine floorboards, and contribute to a warm, bright and spacious interior. Picking out the coving, wall panel mouldings, dado rail and skirting board with a mid-brown hue helps to define the architectural proportions of the room. Pale brown, Crackle-glazed wall panels (see pages 110-11), above and below dado height, break up the surface area and provide contrasting visual interest.*

Above: *A striking, and unusual, Stone Block effect (see pages 100-1), gives the walls of this large dining room a monumental solidity. The painter has successfully varied the size, colour and surface texture of each block, and emphasised the mortar lines with additional shading, to enhance the 'three-dimensional' quality of the finish. The coving, a small column and a decorative arch have all been painted with due reference to correct architectural proportions – and appear all the more authentic for that. Suitably grand accessories – gold candelabra and a brass ring — provide an appropriate finishing touch.*

more airy atmosphere, thereby visually increasing the sense of space; while the former would make the room feel warmer, but the walls seem closer. (For guidance on this, see *The Use of Colour*, pages 90-3).

In recent years there has been, in some quarters, a move away from the 'fitted look', and a return to a more traditional layout in the kitchen and kitchen/ diner. Cast-iron ranges; ceramic sinks; wooden tables doubling-up as work surfaces; free-standing storage cupboards, dressers and electrical appliances; and open racks of pots, pans, vegetables and all manner of cooking utensils etc. . . . a disparate collection of functional, edible and decorative objects, combined in an harmonious, if eclectic, whole.

In this style of interior any finish, or combination of finishes, carried over large areas, such as the walls, ceiling or floor, should provide an unobtrusive background to the main objects of attention – the kitchen appliances themselves. Therefore, subtle finishes such as Watered Silk (see pages 106-7), Tiffany (see pages 118-9), Plaster (see pages 104-5), Porphyry (see pages 102-3) and Two-Colour Distressing (see pages 112-3), applied in soft, pale pastel colours, are particularly appropriate alternatives.

Of course, stronger colours and more strident compositions can be used. But as they will be making yet further demands on the visual sense of space, they are usually best confined to individual objects and

Right: *The classical proportions of this kitchen dresser have been accentuated by employing lighter and darker of shades of an Antiqued finish (see pages 108-9) on the door panels, framework and shelving. This is further enhanced by picking out the quadrant moulding and routed framework around the panels in a contrasting deep burgundy.*

Below: *To decorate the panels, a light blue eggshell glaze was applied over a dark blue one, and then rubbed back (see Antiquing, pages 108-9) to allow the darker glaze to ghost through in patches. The burgundy-coloured mouldings were 'aged' using the same method.*

smaller surfaces. Thus, a large, free-standing fridge might be highlighted in a bold Blazer effect (see pages 116-7), or a large, plain cupboard or dresser picked out in a striking combination of verdigris and copper Metal Patina effects (see pages 96-7).

A similar approach to the use of colour and composition should be adopted when choosing a decorative scheme for a separate dining room. In other words, if it occupies a small, poorly lit space it is better to use lighter colours and more restful finishes, such as Watered Silk (see pages 106-7) or Tiffany (see pages 118-9), over the main surfaces, to alleviate any sense of confinement. Whereas in a large, high-ceilinged room there is scope for employing darker, warmer colours and bolder, more dramatic finishes such as Blazer, Nebula (see pages 122-3) or Lapis Lazuli (see pages 98-9).

But over and above these considerations of light, space and architectural proportion, the dining room, as the setting for dinner parties, if for nothing else, should be something of a showcase in the home – providing an uplifting atmosphere, conducive to eating and conversation, and a decorative scheme that is a feast for the eyes . . . in which case Beast (see pages 120-1) or Aquarium (see pages 114-5) might be the most appropriate finish for the walls!

Left: *A pale pink, fantasy Plaster effect on the walls (see pages 104-5) offsets an Antiqued blue dresser (see pages 108-9), in this farmhouse kitchen. The pastel colours and gently scrubbed texture complement the off-white flagstone floor.*

Above: *An Antiqued Watered Silk effect provides an attractive finish for the panelled doors of kitchen cupboards (for techniques, refer to pages 106-9).*

4

chapter four

bedrooms

BEDROOMS ARE USUALLY CONSIDERED TO BE
private areas in which to rest, relax and indulge in,
at the very least, decorative fantasies – giving
your imagination free rein to choose a scheme
in which little or no concession need be made
to the decor elsewhere in the home, the vagaries
of fashion, or anything else other than
your own sense of style.

It is particularly important when choosing a decorative scheme for a bedroom, more so than for any other room in the house, to make an assessment of colours, finishes, fabrics, etc., *in situ*, under both natural and artificial light. As considerable time may be spent with the curtains drawn and low levels of lighting, it would be disappointing to have mixed and applied coloured glazes which, for example, appeared agreeably faded and mellow in the daytime, but became unacceptably dark and brooding at night.

In addition to the qualities of light, the decorative scheme that you choose will be to some extent determined by the size and scale of the room in question. For example, some finishes, such as Lapis Lazuli (see pages 98-9) and Nebula (see pages 122-3), if carried over large areas like the walls, while looking spectacular in a medium or large-sized room, might prove overbearing in a small cottage one.

This is not to say that small bedrooms automatically prohibit the use of dramatic compositions and saturated, vibrant colours. Rather that, regardless of any particular style you are trying to create, the presence of large items of furniture, such as beds, wardrobes (free-standing or fitted) and chests of drawers, make great

Right: *Contrasting Plaster effects (see pages 104-5) have been successfully combined on adjacent bedroom walls to provide a restful, unobtrusive backdrop for the mahogany furniture and soft furnishings. The natural plaster finish co-ordinates with colours throughout the rest of the decor and, together with the stained and polished floorboards, creates a feeling of warmth, while the pastel green plaster matches the canvas-backed chair, and introduces a cooler note.*

demands on the limited space, which the decorative scheme should attempt to alleviate, rather than add to.

For example, you might use a combination of green and yellow hues in a Two-Colour Distressed finish (see pages 112-3), or a pastiche of a Plaster effect (see pages 104-5), on the walls of a small bedroom overlooking a garden. And by carrying the effect over items such as the bedhead, wardrobe and dressing table (provided they aren't valuable antiques!), rather than leaving them in a strongly contrasting finish (as natural wood, for example), you will blend them into the background, and make them appear smaller and less cumbersome than they actually are. This doesn't mean that everything has to match exactly – obviously the glazes can be adjusted as necessary to create subtle gradations of colour over different surfaces.

In a small bedroom, more strident finishes should be used sparingly – perhaps only employed to feature individual items. Thus a Beast finish (see pages 120-1) on a bedspread or chair cushions would make a dramatic contrast set against soft, off-white pastel colours sponged over the other surfaces. As would Watered Silk panels on the wardrobe doors (see pages 106-7), or a Blazer finish (see pages 116-7) over

Above: *Illuminated by a Lalique glass lamp, the wall shown in this detail has been decorated with an understated Blazer finish (see pages 116-7) in which a coral-coloured glaze has been sponged out over a pale yellow ground coat.*

Left: *A natural Plaster finish (see pages 104-5) has been painted onto the walls of this modern bedroom, and effectively combined with polished woodblock flooring, white cotton bedlinen and drapes, decorative blue panelling and a black and gray rug to create a cool, stylish and uncluttered interior. Halogen lighting enhances the sense of space, and emphasises the subtle gradations of colour and lightly scrubbed texture of the Plaster paintwork.*

Above: *The gently curving walls of this 1930s oval bedroom have been sympathetically decorated with a very subtle Two-Coloured Distressed effect (see pages 112-3). The pale brown glazes in the finish were chosen to unobtrusively co-ordinate with the brown and yellow hues in the walnut veneer wardrobe doors and the bird's eye maple bedhead.*

Above: The soft glow of a bedside uplighter reveals the depth and gently swirling movement in the Nebula finish (see pages 122-3) on the wall behind. The cushions have been decorated using the Porphyry (see pages 102-3) and Aquarium techniques (see pages 114-5).

Right: The semi-opaque panels of this unusual wardrobe have been given a Metal Patina – Lead finish (see variations, page 97). The gray eggshell glazes used to create the effect were chosen to co-ordinate with the rug, chair and wall finish, and contrast with the bright red desk. The gray finish on the wall can be reproduced by introducing a strident diagonal note into the technique for simulating plaster (see pages 104-5).

Far right: Although dramatic in appearance, a swirling Nebula finish (see pages 122-3) can provide a suitably restful decorative treatment for a bedroom ceiling.

a small chest of drawers.

Larger bedrooms provide greater scope for dramatic statements and epic compositions, although it should always be borne in mind that frenetic markings and striking contrasts may not contribute to what ought to be a restful atmosphere. Indeed, as a considerable amount of time is spent reclining, the gentle, almost hypnotic swirls of pale blue Lapis Lazuli (see pages 98-9) carried over the ceiling would be very appropriate, as would the cloudy depths of Nebula (see pages 122-3), providing an inspirational backdrop for contemplation, or simply staring at the ceiling! Obviously both finishes, especially the latter, will visually lower the height of the room to some extent. But that is often no bad thing in a large bedroom, where over-high ceilings can make the room seem colder than it really is.

If you intend to use different finishes, and therefore different patterns, on surfaces in close proximity, it is often a good idea to employ colours of a similar hue

Right: *In this detail, the ultramarine and gold veining of a fantasy Lapis Lazuli wall finish (see pages 98-9) provides a glittering backdrop for a gold-plated cherub chandelier. The combination of gold metal leaf and cloudy gradations of colour can give the surface of a Lapis finish an almost 'three-dimensional' appearance when viewed under certain lights and from various angles.*

Opposite right: *A cloudier, less strident Lapis Lazuli effect (again see pages 98-9) has been painted over the ceiling of this small bedroom. Far less gold metal flake has been used than in the example above, resulting in a softer more restful finish – which, when combined with plain white walls and a lace bedspread and curtains, might well prove more conducive to sleep! Of course, the most eye-catching feature is the splendid* trompe l'oeil baldacchino *– the billowing folds of which complement the gently swirling Lapis, and introduce a dreamlike quality into the decor.*

and tonality (see the advice on using colour, pages 90-3) in each finish, to ensure they work harmoniously together. Thus a light Nebula (see pages 122-3) on the ceiling could be run into a Tiffany effect (see pages 118-9) on the walls, which employed tints and shades of the same blues – the latter being picked up on soft furnishings such as the bedspread and/or curtains.

On the other hand, exciting results can be produced by taking the same finish over a number of surfaces, but changing the hues on each. For example, a pale blue Watered Silk finish (see pages 106-7) could be applied around the walls, and an ivory or pale yellow version of the same effect carried over the ceiling, with additional *trompe l'oeil* rents and billows. This might be combined with a *baldacchino* over the head of the bed; the former draped with raw silk, net or *voile*, and complementing a Watered Silk effect on the head-board and a real silk bedspread.

A bigger bedroom also allows you to use bolder finishes, like Blazer (see pages 116-7), Beast (see pages 120-1) or Metal Patina (see pages 96-7), on large pieces of furniture such as trunks and wardrobes – lending them an impressive monumentality that often sits well in spacious surroundings.

So, at the end of the day, apart from avoiding discordant colours and jarring contrasts, there are few restrictions on the finishes you can employ. Indeed, whether you confront yourself with Beast or cocoon yourself in Nebula, will probably depend on how easy you find it to get to sleep . . .

chapter five

bathrooms

WHEN CHOOSING A DECORATIVE SCHEME
for a bathroom it is important to note that over
and above their function as spaces in which to
wash, shave, make-up etc., bathrooms can be
used as quiet retreats – providing restful yet
inspirational surroundings in which to lie back,
contemplate and wind down from the stresses of
the world outside.

In most homes bathrooms occupy a comparatively small area, often around 4 sq yards/metres or less. Into this space must be squeezed the obligatory three- or four-piece bathroom suite; which in turn is usually accompanied by additional items such as towel rails, vanity units and airing cupboards.

In these circumstances the decorative scheme that you choose should help to alleviate any sense of clutter and confinement, while increasing the sense of space as much as is possible. In most cases this can be achieved by combining pale colours with 'quieter', less stridently composed finishes, and strategically placed mirrors.

For example, a pale Porphyry finish (see pages 102-3) could be carried over all surfaces, including the suite (boxed-in or free-standing), roller blinds, and any tiling. To add visual interest, the suite might be subtly picked out in tints and shades of the colours used on the walls and elsewhere. (Please note that

Above: *An Aquarium finish (see pages 114-5), comprising a cloudy, pale blue background, together with silver, darker blue and coral pink shapes, suggests an aquatic motif that seems entirely appropriate for a bathroom.*

Left: *In this detail, pale brown glazes create a 'fossilized' Aquarium effect (see pages 114-5). A contrasting blue dado rail divides lighter and darker toned versions of the finish. And clear varnish provides invisible protection against water and steam.*

Right: *A pink fantasy Plaster effect (see pages 104-5) has been applied over the (real) textured plaster of these bathroom walls to create a warm, light and airy interior. A contrasting, Antiqued pastel green wall mirror (see pages 108-9) completes the picture.*

Left: *Painters Paul and Janet Czainski have applied a fine Porphyry effect (for technique, see pages 102-3) over the walls and ceiling of this bathroom. The predominant hues of yellow, pale brown and gray used in the finish take their cue from the metallic fittings, and the marbled worktop, architrave and skirtingboard. This combination of colours establishes a feeling of warmth – which is often desirable in a high-ceilinged bathroom.*

Right: *The other end of the bathroom shown opposite clearly reveals how successfully the Porphyry finish has been combined with a marbled bath panel and splashback – the latter displaying simple* trompe l'oeil *panelling. Moreover, using a light gray glaze, the painters have highlighted the divisions between different sections of the walls and ceiling, to again create a simple panel-like effect.*

epoxy-based paints, suitable for ceramic surfaces, are now available in a limited range of colours from various specialist paint suppliers – always carefully follow manufacturers' instructions regarding preparation of surfaces and application.)

Alternatively, the suite, tiling, and possibly the door and surrounding architrave, could be featured in the Porphyry finish (see pages 102-3), with a softly contrasting Plaster effect (see pages 104-5) applied over the walls and ceiling – the glazes being either lightened or darkened over the latter if there is any need to visually heighten or lower it, and thereby adjust the proportions of the room.

Of course you may prefer to leave the bathroom suite and other fittings undecorated, in the colours the manufacturer intended. Plainly a white suite is the most versatile – placing no restriction on the colours you might like to use elsewhere in the room, while

coloured suites in shades of blue and green allow you to use hues that reflect the use of water. With this in mind the Aquarium finish (see pages 114-5) carried around the walls, and offset by a white or very pale blue ceiling, would provide a wholly appropriate and harmonious contrast. Moreover, the composition can be adjusted to alter the balance of movement and tranquility in the finish, according to taste; while the silver cast of the 'fish scales' will echo any chrome fittings, and the soft pink and coral coloured 'shoals' of tiny 'fish' introduce a warmer note.

The finishes suggested thus far for smaller bathrooms will work equally well when employed over larger areas, though bigger, naturally lighter, bathrooms – especially those, often found in older houses, which have been converted from bedrooms – do offer greater scope for using darker colours, stronger contrasts and bolder compositions. For example, a

Plaster finish (see pages 104-5) on the walls could be combined with *trompe l'oeil* Stone Block arches (see pages 100-1), and offset by a suite finished in Porphyry (see pages 102-3), in a pastiche of a Roman bath house. Or, for a more restful decor, an iridescent Tiffany finish (see pages 118-9), employing three or four soft pastel colours, including one matched to the suite, might be carried around the walls and contrasted with flat-painted or sponged doors and mouldings, also in the colour of the suite.

Larger bathrooms also give you the option of featuring particular items and areas in a style that in a more confined setting might appear overbearing. For example, if there are no tiles already *in situ* around the bath or hand basin, you could adapt the grid technique employed for making a Stone Block effect (see pages 100-1) to create a *trompe l'oeil* tile splashback. Onto this might be stencilled a nautical motif, followed by a Crackle glaze (see pages 110-11), to create a crazed, aged surface – an effect that could be echoed by Antiquing (see pages 108-9) other surfaces, such as the doors, elsewhere in the room. Or you might like to pick out the radiator and any exposed pipework in Verdigris (see pages 96-7). (Of course, if you leave copper pipes and brass fittings exposed for long enough, damp and condensation will do the work for you!).

But whatever finishes you employ in a bathroom, it is very important to protect the glazes, even the tougher oil-based eggshells, from the adverse effects of water, steam and condensation, by applying one or two coats of clear varnish. However, some varnishes will slightly darken and enrich certain colours, and this should be borne in mind when mixing glazes. (For guidance on varnishing, see page 89.)

Left: *A subtle blend of pastel yellow, orange and white glazes has been applied to these bathroom walls, using a Plaster technique (see pages 104-5). Picking up colour from the bathroom suite and beech block floor, the wall finish helps to create a warm, bright, co-ordinated interior, and provides an unobtrusive backdrop for displaying numerous decorative objects. In relatively small areas choosing a compositionally understated finish like Plaster (or Tiffany, see pages 118-9), and mixing the glazes to co-ordinate with colours used elsewhere in the decor, will help to maximize a sense of spaciousness – often all too limited in a bathroom.*

Far left: *In this detail, gray, black and white glazes have been used to create an elegant Porphyry effect (see pages 102-3) over the bathroom walls. The finish – which complements the vase and has also been applied to one of the small containers – provides a particularly suitable backdrop for the pristine white basin and expensive chrome fittings, while the colours have been carefully chosen to co-ordinate with the vanitory unit doors, framed prints and the toiletries. A coat of clear satin varnish protects the Porphyry finish from splashes and steam.*

Above: *Pale olive-green and yellow glazes (colours found in the ceramic floor tiles) have been employed to create a Two-Colour Distressed finish on the textured plaster walls of this sunny bathroom.*
Near right: *A pale gray Porphyry finish (see pages 102-3) applied around the sides of a traditional-style free-standing bath looks especially authentic. A simple Stone Block effect (see pages 100-1), carried over the wall and floor, completes the picture.*

Far right: *A soft gray Stone Block effect (again see pages 100-1) frames the recessed bath, and* *provides a neutral contrast to the yellow onyx marbled panelling, in this elegant interior.*

chapter six

furniture and small objects

QUITE ORDINARY PIECES OF FURNITURE and otherwise insignificant decorative objects can be dramatically transformed into highly prized *objets d'arts* by giving them a Fantasy Finish. Alternatively, hopelessly unattractive items can be disguised, and blended into the surrounding decor. In both cases, decorative painting allows you to visually adjust the lines, proportions and scale of an object so that it enhances rather than diminishes its surroundings.

With the obvious exclusion of valuable antiques, both traditional and modern pieces of furniture provide many suitable subjects for decorative paint finishes. However, before proceeding, it is important to make an initial assessment of the object in relation to the surrounding decor. For instance, in a small cottage bedroom a large, rather cumbersome wardrobe, veneered in a dark oak, might appear overbearing. In which case, blending it into the surrounding walls by applying, for example, a pale Two-Coloured Distressed finish (see pages 112-3) over both surfaces would make less demands on the sense of space, while giving the wardrobe a dramatically different appearance.

As with the wardrobe, taking a decorative finish over the entire surface of a piece of furniture will tend to resolve any particular features, such as panelling or carved mouldings, into an amorphous whole. If the object has an ugly or indifferent construction this may be no bad thing. However, where you find the lines and proportions particularly pleasing, you may wish to accentuate or emphasise them. For example, the panelled doors of a wardrobe or bookcase could be 'lined' with a Watered Silk finish (see pages 106-7), which could in turn be Antiqued (see pages 108-9) to simulate a faded elegance that might be picked up on doors and mouldings elsewhere in the room.

If you are to disguise a piece of furniture or decorative object, reducing its presence and blending it into its surroundings, the colours and composition you use must obviously match those on the adjacent surfaces. However, if you have decided to highlight the

Left: *Set against a Metal Patina (see pages 96-7) and muted Lapis Lazuli (see pages 98-9) backdrop, this wooden table lamp has been given a reddy-brown Porphyry finish (see pages 102-3) which complements the elaborate, bronzed wrought iron frame of the daybed. The shade, echoing the blues and sandy-yellow colours in the soft furnishings, has been decorated with a Metal Patina technique (see pages 96-7).*
Right: *The wooden framework of this mirror-backed display cabinet has been given a subtle, pale blue Crackle-glazed finish (see pages 110-11). Various methods of controlling the depth and extent of the crazing can be employed.*

Above: *The application of a pale Verdigris finish (see pages 96-7) ensures the large wooden cross dominates this hallway. As the wrought iron chair ages, it will probably play host to the real effects of oxidation!*

Right: *A subtle light and dark green Crackle finish (see pages 110-11) has been employed to give this small wooden obelisk the appearance of aged and weathered decorative stone.*

Right: *Smallbone Furniture have tastefully decorated this magnificent breakfront desk and bookcase with a pale green distressed finish (see Antiquing, pages 108-9). When embellishing elegant pieces such as this, it is usually best to 'age' them with discretion – only going 'over the top' with less formal items.*

Note that the plaster bust above has been lent additional weight and solidity by being given a weathered bronze – Verdigris finish (see pages 96-7).

piece, or parts of it, it is equally important to choose colours and a finish that provides an appropriate and harmonious contrast with the background. Thus, a chest of drawers might be decorated with a Beast finish (see pages 120-1), and become the dramatic focal point of the room, if offset by a soft gray Porphyry effect (see pages 102-3) on the surrounding walls. However, set against a dark red and black Blazer finish (see pages 116-7), it would simply look garish and the colours would probably clash. (For guidance on the use of colour, see pages 90-3).

Of course, just as the particular finish you choose must relate to the background, so it should be appropriate to the object itself. For example, you might wish to redecorate a modern coffee table to both feature in, and co-ordinate with, a new decorative scheme. Applying a fine Crackle glaze (see pages 110-11), and rubbing in an artists' oil in a hue found on surfaces elsewhere in the room, would achieve this objective,

without altering the elegant lines and proportions of the table (though the top should be protected with a plain sheet of glass). On the other hand, if you were to apply a dark Porphyry finish (see pages 102-3), the table would appear a heavier, cruder piece of furniture altogether.

Of course, avoiding overly-strong contrasts is less of a problem with relatively small objects, such as jewellery boxes, plant pots, vases, or table lamps, which can be embellished with stronger and more vibrant colours and finishes that might appear over-bearing over larger areas. Thus, in a small bedroom, a jewellery box might be finished in a swirling dark blue and gold Lapis Lazuli effect (see pages 98-9); whereas if the same effect were taken over the walls and ceiling it would certainly close down the space, and might prove unconducive to sleeping. In other words, the smaller the object, the greater the scope for employing a striking finish, and the less likelihood of it clashing with the surrounding decor.

chapter seven

techniques – the basics

THE FOLLOWING SECTION COVERS THE PREPARATION
of surfaces, details the paints and glazes used in
decorative painting – showing how they can be prepared
and advising on their suitability for various surfaces and
types of finish – and lists the tools, brushes and equipment
that will be required. In addition there is an introduction to
the various properties of colour – suggesting how these
can be exploited to produce different effects – and advice
on how to work successfully over large areas.

The preparation of surfaces

The successful appearance and durability of any Fantasy Finish is heavily dependent on the condition of the underlying surface – whether it be plaster, wood, melamine or metal, painted or unpainted. You cannot expect translucent glazes to disguise chips, lumpy repairs, ugly brushmarks and paint misses; or survive for long on top of flaking paint, damp plaster, resinous wood knots or rust. Consequently, for the best results, you are encouraged to adopt a diligent approach to the preparatory stage of decorative painting, as explained over the following pages.

Bare plaster

If oil-based paints and glazes are to be used to create the Fantasy Finish, then smooth, undamaged new plaster should first be sealed with a proprietary primer as instructed on the tin. When this has dried, at least one opaque oil-based undercoat should be applied, preferably with a smooth roller, prior to the application of the specified eggshell. Alternatively, for finishes such as the Plaster effect (see pages 104-5), where water-based paints and glazes are used, prime with watered-down, matt finish emulsion (latex), followed by one or two unthinned, opaque coats of matt or silk finish emulsion. Old but sound bare plaster should be treated as above.

Any loose, or 'live', plaster should be removed with a scraper, and holes and cracks cleaned out, dusted down and their edges chamfered with coarse grade sandpaper or a craft knife. After the surrounding area has been abraded with medium grade sandpaper, the hole or crack should be filled to just proud of the surface using a proprietary filler (always follow the manufacturer's instructions). When this has thoroughly dried out, the surface should be levelled using medium grade sandpaper. Minor imperfections can be corrected with the application of a fine grade surface filler (spackle), and then rubbed down with fine grade sandpaper. Finally, undercoat or emulsion should be applied, as above. Of course, minor imperfections and patched-in sections of plaster can be quite successfully disguised by covering the walls with lining paper. (For preparation use the same method as for wallpaper.)

It should be pointed out that while finishes such as Tiffany (see pages 118-9) and Watered Silk (see pages 106-7) require very smooth surfaces to be fully effective others, such as Plaster (see pages 104-5) and Porphyry (see pages 102-3), can accommodate minor imperfections, like fine cracks, in their composition, as part of the illusion. Indeed, in a Stone Block finish (see pages 100-1) you might wish to paint in *trompe l'oeil* cracks if they weren't already there! So, the degree to which you pursue 'perfection' in the underlying surface can be partly determined by the type of Fantasy Finish you intend to create.

Painted plaster

Sound painted surfaces should be washed down with warm soapy water and a little disinfectant, to remove any dust, dirt and grease, and then thoroughly rinsed with clean water. If there is evidence of mould a proprietary fungicide should be added to the wash, following manufacturer's instructions. (Oil-based gloss and eggshell should then be keyed with medium grade wet-and-dry paper.) Once dry, the surface should be painted with one or two coats of either oil-based undercoat or matt or silk finish emulsion (latex), depending on the type of glazes to be used in the Fantasy Finish (see *Bare Plaster* left).

You should note that some colours in painted surfaces may be unstable, especially reds, and bleed through superimposed undercoats or emulsions. If this happens you will need to apply aluminium primer (available from specialist decorator outlets) before applying the undercoat or emulsion.

Small areas of flaking or bubbling paint should be rubbed down, and the edges feathered, with medium grade sandpaper. After the application of a proprietary surface sealer/stabilizer (following manufacturer's instructions), the indented surface must be levelled with fine grade surface filler (spackle) and a plastic spreader. And when dry, it should be smoothed down with fine grade wet-and-dry or sandpaper and re-sealed, before the application of undercoat or emulsion, as above.

If the flaking or bubbling paint is widespread, a more practical method of achieving a smooth finish is to rub it down and seal it, as above. And then cover the entire surface with lining paper, prior to priming and undercoating.

Wallpaper

Embossed, badly damaged or peeling wallpaper must be stripped, and the underlying plaster repaired and prepared as in *Bare Plaster* left. However, if the paper is smooth and in good condition it should be gently wiped down with warm, soapy water and disinfectant, rinsed, and when thoroughly dry sealed either with thinned oil-based undercoat or emulsion (latex paint) prior to the application of one or two coats of unthinned undercoat or emulsion (latex paint), again as in *Bare Plaster*, see left.

Please note that vinyl wallpapers are unsuitable for emulsion ground coats, but can be prepared with oil-based undercoats.

Concrete floors

Major surface repairs may be effected with self-levelling screeds (available from builders' merchants – follow manufacturer's instructions). Smaller holes and cracks can be repaired with proprietary fillers, as in *Bare Plaster* opposite. When the floor has thoroughly dried out, the application of one or two coats of linoleum paint (available from DIY outlets) will provide a smooth, non-porous ground suitable for a Fantasy Finish.

Vinyl flooring

It must be said that sheet vinyl and vinyl tiles present a major problem as far as preparation is concerned. The difficulty is in keying the surface. If you do decide to decorate them, follow the method outlined below (and preferably experiment first on a spare tile or flooring offcut). But be warned, there is no guarantee that the finish will stick! Provided it is in good condition, vinyl flooring should be thoroughly washed with hot soapy water to remove dirt and grease, allowed to dry, roughed up with coarse or medium grade sandpaper and then sealed with a proprietary polyurethane sealant (available from DIY outlets – follow manufacturer's instructions), prior to undercoating as in *Bare Plaster* opposite.

Ceramic tiles

As a suitable ground for Fantasy Finishes ceramic tiles have the same limitations as *Vinyl Flooring* above, and must be prepared in a similar manner, prior to sealing with a proprietary ceramic sealant (available from DIY outlets).

Floorboards

Obviously, the strong directional accent of the boards will become a prominent feature in any Fantasy Finish. If you wish to decorate them, they should be prepared in the same manner as wooden doors, mouldings and furniture – see *Painted Wooden Surfaces,* opposite and *Waxed, Shellacked* and *Bare Wooden Surfaces* overleaf.

Hardboard

Painted hardboard panels, such as those often used to box-in the sides of baths, should be prepared in the same way as sound *Painted Plaster*, for method see opposite. However, bare hardboard must first be primed with a proprietary hardboard sealant (available from specialist decorators' outlets and builders'

merchants), or thinned emulsion (latex paint), prior to undercoating.

Glass

The surface should be washed down with soapy water to remove dirt and grease, rinsed with clean water, and then dried thoroughly. After abrading the glass with medium grade wet-and-dry or sandpaper, two or three oil-based undercoats will need to be applied to establish an opaque surface suitable for the eggshell ground specified in the Fantasy Finish.

Metal surfaces

Sound painted metal surfaces should be prepared in the same way as *Painted Plaster* opposite. However, badly chipped and flaking paint and any evidence of rust must be removed:

1 Put on goggles and rubber (household) gloves to protect eyes and hands.
2 Open the windows and doors to improve ventilation and allow unpleasant fumes to escape.
3 Brush on several coats of spirit-based chemical paint stripper.
4 As the paint blisters, scrape it off with a wire brush and grade 1 or 2 wire (steel) wool.
5 Treat any rust with several coats of proprietary rust inhibitor (available from DIY outlets).
6 Apply a coat of metal primer.
7 Apply one or two coats of oil-based undercoat. (Do not use emulsion, as it will encourage rust.)

Melamine or laminate-faced chipboard

Kitchen unit doors are often faced with melamine or plastic laminate. They should be prepared in the same way as sound *Painted Plaster* opposite, but it is especially important to thoroughly key the surface with coarse grade wet-and-dry paper before the application of undercoat.

Painted wooden surfaces

Sound painted wooden surfaces, and those with minor damage, should be prepared in the same way as *Painted Plaster* opposite – the only difference being that exposed areas of bare wood should be sealed with a thinned coat of PVA adhesive or white glue (available from DIY outlets) prior to the application of a proprietary fine grade filler (spackle), exposed knots should be re-sealed with proprietary knotting compound (available from DIY outlets), and when dry the repaired areas should be primed with thinned emulsion (latex paint) before undercoating.

On the other hand, painted wooden surfaces on

which flaking or peeling is widespread must be stripped back to the bare wood:

1 Put on goggles and rubber (household) gloves to protect eyes and hands.

2 Open the windows and doors to improve ventilation and allow unpleasant fumes to escape.

3 Brush on several coats of spirit-based chemical stripper (don't use water-based, as it may raise the grain of the wood).

4 When the paint begins to soften and blister, scrape it away with a stripping knife and grade 0 or 1 wire (steel) wool, taking care not to damage the underlying wood, and applying further coats of stripper as necessary. Use an old toothbrush to clear the debris from any relief mouldings.

5 When all the paint has been stripped off, rub down the bare wood with white spirit (mineral spirits) and a rag to remove fine debris and neutralize any remnants of the chemical stripper.

6 Now follow the instructions for preparing *Bare Wooden Surfaces*, see below.

Waxed and oiled wooden surfaces

Wax and oil must be removed prior to painting. Rub down the surface with white spirit (mineral spirits) and grade 00 wire (steel) wool, in the direction of the wood grain, until the wax and oil dissolve. Finish off by wiping over the surface with a clean cloth and then follow the instructions for preparing *Bare Wooden Surfaces*, see below.

Shellacked and varnished surfaces

Sound surfaces can be prepared in the same way as sound *Painted Plaster* (see page 72). However, damaged shellac must be removed with methylated spirits (denatured alcohol) and grade 00 wire (steel) wool, while flaking cellulose-based varnishes should be got rid of with spirit-based chemical paint stripper (see *Metal Surfaces*, page 73). Then, in both cases, follow the instructions for preparing *Bare Wooden Surfaces*, see below.

Bare wooden surfaces

Having removed flaking and peeling paint, varnish, wax and oil from a wooden surface you will need to:

1 Cover any nail or screw heads exposed just below the surface with a minimum of two coats of metal primer.

2 Fill gaps or holes with a flexible wood filler (spackle), following the manufacturer's instructions regarding whether or not you need to prime the wood first.

3 By the time the filler has dried out it will have contracted to below the height of the surrounding area. Apply a generous layer of fine grade filler (spackle) on top, and when that has dried rub it, and the entire surface, down with fine grade sandpaper to create a smooth, level finish.

4 Cover any exposed knots with a minimum of two coats of white knotting compound.

5 Apply one coat of white, oil-based wood primer over the entire surface. Then allow the primer to dry thoroughly.

6 Apply one or two oil-based undercoats prior to the application of the eggshell ground specified in the Fantasy Finish.

Fabrics

There are a number of steps and precautions you must follow before (and after) painting fabrics:

1. Wash, rinse and press the cloth before you paint it. This will remove any chemical finish in the fabric (which might react adversely with the paint), and prevent shrinkage in subsequent washings – both of which would almost certainly spoil the decorative finish).

2. Whenever possible use natural fabrics such as cotton or linen, as paints don't adhere or perform as well on man-made synthetics.

3. Before painting, stretch the fabric out over a slightly padded but flat suface (you could use an old blanket over a table or worktop), and secure it in place with low-tack masking tape.

4. If you don't have enough space to stretch a large piece of fabric (such as a bedspread) right out, partly fold it and paint it in sections. But do make sure that each section is thoroughly dry before starting on the next one – otherwise it will smudge and ruin the finish. And do spend some time making sure that the colours and composition of the various sections match up and/or blend in with each other when the fabric is unfolded.

5. You can paint already-made-up fabric items, but if they have a double thickness (eg, a pillow or cushion cover) you must slip a polythene-covered piece of card in between the two layers so that paint from the top layer doesn't seep through to smudge the one below.

6. After painting, but before use, you must 'fix' the finish by covering it with a clean cotton cloth, and then pressing it for a few minutes with a medium-hot iron. This will provide protection against wear and tear and ensure the fabric can be washed at a later date.

7. Finally, always carefully follow any specific instructions given by the fabric paint manufacturer regarding the preparation of surfaces (and preferred methods of application and drying times).

Working over large areas

When working on areas larger than a couple of square yards or metres (such as a long expanse of wall or ceiling), you will be faced with two problems: firstly, that of 'working' the wet glazes over the eggshell ground coat, to create the desired effect before they dry out; and secondly, of blending a wet section of the finish into an adjacent area that has already dried out, without creating a noticeable join between them.

Working method

Ideally, you should have a helper with whom you can split the workload. Thus, for example, while A sponges or brushes on the first glaze, B follows immediately behind, softening and blending the glaze as necessary. That way, you always keep a wet edge. When A finishes, he or she can begin to apply a second glaze, with B following on behind. And so on . . . In addition, it is recommended that A and B combine roles occasionally, as 'working' the glaze can be more time consuming than applying it (for example, see the Tiffany effect, pages 118-9). But make sure that you don't lose the wet edge.

However, if a helper is unavailable you will be unable to keep a wet edge, and therefore must adopt a different approach. Thus, when creating a fantasy finish on the walls of a room, work on one wall at a time (it is best to start with the smallest one). Assuming that you are right-handed, start at the top right-hand corner and apply the first translucent glaze over the eggshell ground coat, working down and across to cover a couple of square yards or metres of the surface.

You must apply the glaze (whether with sponge or brush) so that the edge of the section has an irregular shape that relates to the type of finish you are creating. Thus, for example, Blazer should have a billowing or softly undulating edge (see pages 116-7), while Metal Patina could have a more broken, jagged edge (see pages 96-7). But whatever the shape, it is equally important to sponge or brush out the glaze very thinly along the edges, 'working' it to near complete transparency.

On the other hand, some finishes, such as Plaster (see pages 104-5), Porphyry (see pages 102-3) and Stone Blocking (see pages 100-1), given the nature of the material you are simulating, allow the option of making a feature of joins between sections – jagged or undulating lines can represent cracking across the surface (as shown in the picture on the left).

When you have finished a section, begin on an adjacent area, gradually building up and overlapping the glazes over the dry edges of the first section – using either sponge, stippler or badger softener (whichever tool is specified in each fantasy finish, for 'working' the glaze) to soften and blend the sections together.

Repeat this process of blending irregular-shaped sections together until you have completed the wall. Then proceed to the next one.

Left: *Decorating large expanses of wall or ceiling, as in the drawing room here, can present a problem if you are working on your own. Because it is impossible to keep a wet edge in the glaze as you work across the surface, you must blend new wet sections into ones that have already dried out (for technique, see main text). However, the Plaster finish (see pages 104-5), as shown here, gives you* the option of making a feature of irregular-shaped joins between sections. They can be 'highlighted' with a slightly darker glaze to represent 'realistic' cracks or crazing (or a contrasting colour could be used for a 'fantasy' effect). Of course, for aesthetic reasons you must give some consideration to the composition of the 'cracks' – even if you wish them to appear random!*

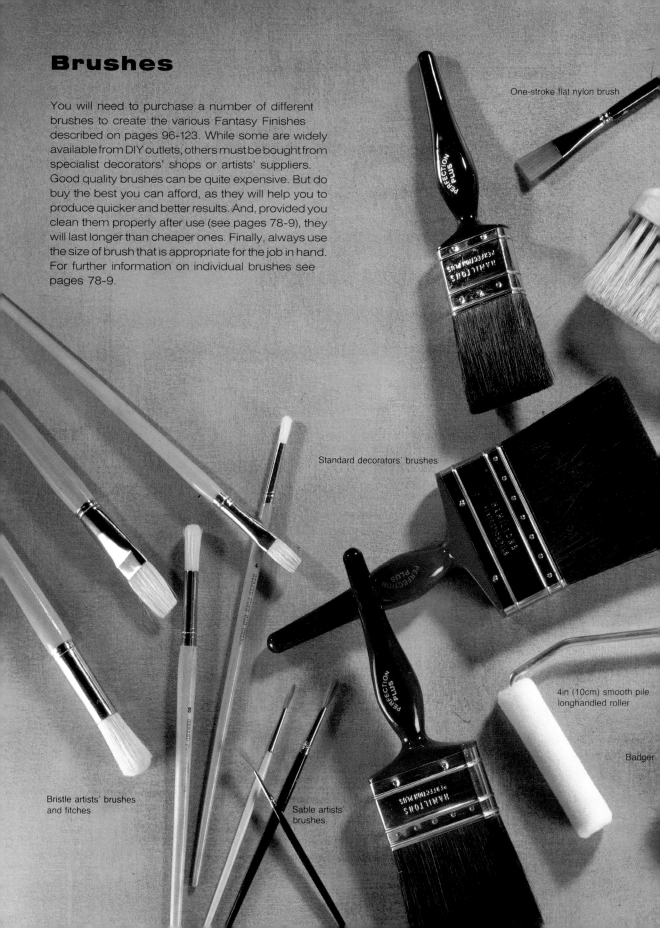

Brushes

You will need to purchase a number of different brushes to create the various Fantasy Finishes described on pages 96-123. While some are widely available from DIY outlets, others must be bought from specialist decorators' shops or artists' suppliers. Good quality brushes can be quite expensive. But do buy the best you can afford, as they will help you to produce quicker and better results. And, provided you clean them properly after use (see pages 78-9), they will last longer than cheaper ones. Finally, always use the size of brush that is appropriate for the job in hand. For further information on individual brushes see pages 78-9.

One-stroke flat nylon brush

Standard decorators' brushes

4in (10cm) smooth pile longhandled roller

Badger

Bristle artists' brushes and fitches

Sable artists' brushes

4 by 1in (10 by 2.5cm)
edge stippler

6 by 1in
(15 by 2.5cm)
edge stippler

Dusting brush

WHISTLER·GLIDER – N°3

9in (22.5cm)
smooth pile roller

4 by 3in (10 by 7.5cm)
stippler

OMEGA

Flat-bristle
varnish brush

Flogger

WHISTLER

6 by 2in (15 by 5cm)
stippler

WHISTLER
PURE BADGER. MADE IN ENGLAND

Thin flat-bristle
brush

OMEGA

STANDARD DECORATORS' BRUSHES: Available from both DIY and specialist outlets, in sizes ranging from 1 in (2.5 cm) through to 6 in (15 cm). They can be used to prime and undercoat surfaces, as well for applying eggshell, flat-oil and emulsion grounds. However, wherever possible the latter should be applied with a smooth pile roller (see below), rather than a standard decorators' brush, as it is difficult to disguise brushmarks, however skilful or careful you are. Obviously this will be impossible over mouldings and small objects – for which a 1 in or 2 in (2.5 cm or 5 cm) brush is ideal. Larger sizes (4 in/10 cm) can provide a cheaper and slightly less effective alternative to a flogger when creating a Watered Silk finish (see pages 106-7).

THIN FLAT-BRISTLED BRUSHES: Otherwise known as 'gliders', these brushes are available in sizes ranging from 1-6 in (2.5-15 cm) from specialist outlets. They hold, and pick up, only small quantities of paint and glaze, and thus are useful for finishes such as Metal Patina (see pages 96-7), in which eggshell glaze must be brushed out sparsely over a ground coat, using a dry brush. They are also used to 'cut into' and

open up glazes, to create the 'weave' in the 'fabric' of Watered Silk (see pages 106-7), and for applying glaze to mouldings.

SMOOTH AND MEDIUM PILE ROLLERS: Available from both DIY and specialist outlets, in 4 in (10 cm), 7 in (17.5 cm) and 9 in (22.5 cm) sizes. They produce a smooth, slightly 'stippled' finish when used to apply coats of eggshell (use a smooth pile roller) or emulsion (use a medium pile roller) over previously prepared surfaces. This provides the ideal ground for most of the translucent glazes used in the Fantasy Finishes, and avoids the potential problem of brushmarks left by standard decorators' brushes.

FLAT AND OVAL VARNISHING BRUSHES: Available from specialist outlets in 1 in (2.5 cm), 2 in (5 cm) and 3 in (7.5 cm) sizes, they have more fine bristles to the square inch (sq cm) than standard decorators' brushes, allowing easier application and a smoother, mark-free finish. They should only be used for varnishing, and always scrupulously cleaned after use.

BADGER SOFTENER: Available from specialist outlets, this fairly expensive soft-bristled brush is indispensable

CLEANING BRUSHES

1. *As soon as you finish work, you should remove oil-based paints, glazes and varnishes (for water-based types see step 2) by thoroughly cleaning the brush in white spirit (mineral spirits) or a proprietary cleaner, using new solvent as often as is necessary, before following the method outlined in steps 3 to 6 (see right).*

2. *As soon as you finish work, you should remove water-based paints and glazes by immediately cleaning the brush in pure soap and warm water (avoid detergents as they tend to dry out the bristles).*

3. *Once the paint is removed from your brush, you must thoroughly rinse out the bristles in clean, cold water. (You may have to repeat step 1 or step 2 if necessary.)*

for softening and blending glazes to create many of the effects used in Fantasy Finishes. Cheaper, hog's hair alternatives are available, but they are harder to use. Again, always clean and dry thoroughly after use.

DUSTING BRUSH: A soft-bristled brush available from DIY outlets and specialist suppliers. It is very useful for removing dust from surfaces just prior to the application of glazes and varnishes, and can, at a pinch, be used to soften and blend glazes if a badger softener is unavailable.

FLOGGER: Available from specialist outlets in a variety of sizes, this fairly expensive, long-bristled brush is used for dragging (see Watered Silk, pages 106-7). Although standard decorators' brushes provide a cheaper alternative, they are harder to use and produce a softer, more 'blurred' drag.

STIPPLERS AND EDGE STIPPLERS: Available from specialist outlets in a variety of sizes, they are used in a number of the Fantasy Finishes to stipple (lift off fine freckles of paint), soften and blend glazes (see for example, Tiffany, pages 118-9). Use 4 in by 3 in (10 cm

by 7.5 cm) and 6 in by 5 in (15 cm by 12.5 cm) sizes on large, flat surfaces such as walls, and 6 in by 1 in (15 cm by 2.5 cm) and 4 in by 1 in (10 cm by 2.5 cm) on mouldings and small objects, and in awkward corners.

ARTISTS' BRUSHES: Available from artists' suppliers in a variety of sizes and different qualities. Soft-bristled sable brushes (sizes 2 to 6) are best for fine details. Buy the best you can afford.

FITCHES: Hog's hair brushes are available from artists' suppliers in a variety of shapes and sizes (flat, oval and angled). They are used for the application of small sections of glaze in finishes such as Beast (see pages 120-1) and Aquarium (see pages 114-5), and can be used for spattering and cissing in, for example, Antiquing (see pages 108-9) and Porphyry (see pages 102-3).

ONE-STROKE FLAT NYLON BRUSH: A small, fine bristled, flat brush (½-1 in/1.25-2 cm) available from artists' suppliers. It is ideal for picking out/lining sections of raised mouldings (see Tiffany, pages 118-9); and for flat *trompe l'oeil* lining (see Plaster, pages 104-5).

 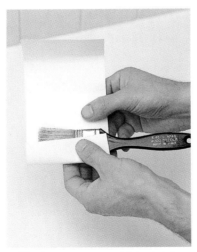 

4. *After rinsing the brush, you should vigorously shake out any excess water from the bristles.*

5. *The best way to avoid the bristles splaying out as they dry is to wrap a sleeve of plain paper around them.*

6. *Hold the sleeve of paper in place with an elastic band. Then let the brush dry out – place it either on its side or bristle-up – at room temperature.*
Note: It is important that you keep brushes well away from fires and radiators, as direct heat may damage them.

Materials

As well as brushes, paints and glazes, various additional items of equipment are needed for the preparation and creation of Fantasy Finishes. Always make sure that you have all the materials you need to hand before you start the job – you don't want to have to break off to visit the store in the middle of your work. Many products can be bought from regular DIY outlets, but some are only available from specialist decorators' and artists' suppliers (see page 124). For further information on individual items see pages 82-3.

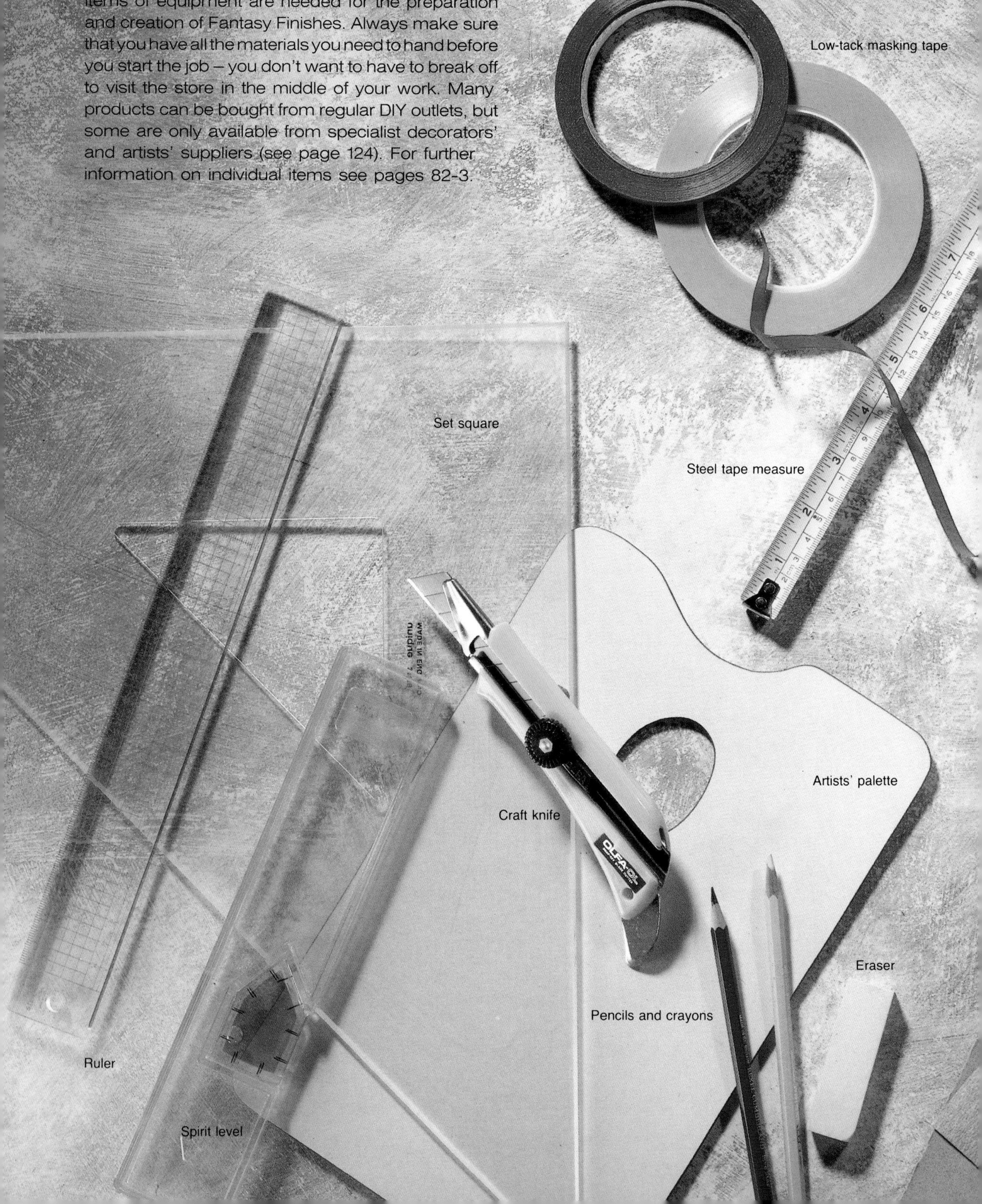

Low-tack masking tape

Set square

Steel tape measure

Craft knife

Artists' palette

Pencils and crayons

Eraser

Ruler

Spirit level

Funnel

Paper filter

Mixing containers

Textured sponge

Spoons

Wet-and-dry and sandpaper

Steel wool

Sanding block

Lint-free cotton rag

Paint tray

Spatula knife

Chemical-resistant rubber gloves

MIXING CONTAINERS: Plastic and alloy paint kettles and mixing bowls, for preparing paints and glazes and cleaning brushes, are widely available in a variety of sizes (1 and 2 litre capacities are best). If you intend to mix your own glazes from scratch, you may need six or seven containers. In addition, a plastic bucket is very useful for tinting large quantities of emulsion or eggshell paint prior to application as a ground coat.

PAINT FILTERS: Plastic funnels and paper filters for straining paints, glazes and varnishes prior to application are available from specialist decorators' suppliers. The filters come in a variety of grades, and you will require a selection in order to strain both thick, viscous paints and varnishes and thinner translucent glazes.

PLASTIC AND METAL SPOONS: Useful for stirring paints, mixing glazes and making the tea.

PAINT TRAY: Used for holding paints and glazes while rolling, brushing or sponging them over a surface – the applicator can be pressed against the raised section of the tray to remove excess paint or glaze.

LINT-FREE COTTON RAG: Lint-free rag available from fabric suppliers.

RUBBER GLOVES: Chemical-resistant rubber gloves are available from hardware stores. Don't use ordinary household gloves, as they will disintegrate in white spirit.

WET AND DRY PAPER: Otherwise known as silicon carbide paper, it is available from DIY outlets. Medium and fine grades can be used to rub down eggshell ground coats, in order to key the surface and remove any small nibs prior to the application of translucent glazes. And, if desired the paper can be used wet, to avoid creating dust and scratching the surface. Fine grade sandpaper (see below) provides a quicker-to-use alternative, but makes it much easier to scratch the surface.

SANDPAPER: Used to smooth rough surfaces prior to the application of undercoat. Can also be used to simulate scuffing and general wear and tear when Antiquing (see pages 108-9).

TEXTURING A SPONGE

Heavyweight, synthetic decorators' sponges, available from all decorators' suppliers, can be 'textured' with scissors or a craft knife to make them suitable for the application of glazes, see right. You should never use them untextured because when they are in unadulterated condition they will leave too regular – and dull – a print.

These synthetic sponges are cheaper and much easier to use than the natural marine sponges that many books on decorative paint techniques recommend. A further disadvantage of marine sponges is that they tend to shrink, stiffen and dry out too quickly when immersed in oil-based glazes and cleaned in white spirit (mineral spirits).

1. *Start by grasping a new synthetic decorators' sponge firmly in one hand.*

2. *Using a craft knife, cut off the hard-edged rectangular perimeter of the sponge in order to make it into an oval shape.*

SANDING BLOCK: Used with above to create a smooth surface.

WIRE WOOL: Available in grades 000-0 (the former is the finest). It is more flexible than wet and dry paper, and is therefore useful for rubbing down curved mouldings, both prior to painting and while Antiquing (see pages 108-9). Sometimes known as steel wool.

ARTISTS' PALETTE: Available from artists' suppliers, and used for mixing small quantities of artists' oils when composing a finish such as Beast (see pages 120-1).

PENCILS AND WATER-BASED CRAYONS: Used to draw the outlines of stone blocks (see pages 100-1) and *trompe l'oeil* features (see pages 104-5).

ERASER: For removing pencil outlines after paint and glazes have been applied.

LOW-TACK MASKING TAPE: Available from specialist decorators' outlets and artists' suppliers. Use 5mm widths to mask off adjacent stone blocks from each other and establish grout lines (see pages 100-1). Much wider widths (1 in/2.5 cm) can be used to mask off and protect areas adjacent to those you are decorating. Being low-tack there is far less risk of paint, or even plaster, being pulled off when the tape is removed.

STEEL TAPE MEASURE: Used to measure up surfaces for the Stone Block finish (see pages 100-1), and to assess surface area when deciding how much paint or glaze you will need.

SPIRIT LEVEL: Used to establish true horizontals and verticals when drawing up the pencil grid for a Stone Block finish (see pages 100-1).

SET SQUARE: Used to establish 90 degree angles for the Stone Block finish (see pages 100-1).

PERSPEX RULER: To assist in drawing straight lines.

CRAFT KNIFE OR SCISSORS: Useful for cutting masking tape or texturing a decorator's sponge (see below).

3. *Again using the craft knife, slightly bevel the edge of the face of the sponge. This is to ensure that the sponge doesn't leave a uniform outline on the surface when you use it to apply glazes.*

4. *Next, using either sharp-pointed scissors or a craft knife, rip out small pieces from the face of the sponge. The size and proximity of the rips can be adjusted to suit the type of 'print' you wish to make.*

5. *Obviously, both sides of the sponge can be textured to different degrees if required.*

Paints and glazes

Proprietary paints, glazes and varnishes are available from DIY shops and artists' and specialist decorators' suppliers, in a wide range of colours and formulations; as are the basic ingredients for mixing your own glazes. (For further information, and for advice on preparing a basic palette of artists' oils, see pages 84-93.)

Japan gold size

Linseed oil

Dutch metal transfer leaf

Water-based emulsion (latex) paint

Metallic paint

Fluorescent eggshell paint

White undercoat

Oil-based eggshell paint

Water-based varnish

Oil-based varnish

Scumble glaze

White (mineral) spirit

Artists' oils

Artists' acrylic colours

Artists' palette

Paint is the traditional medium for applying colour to surfaces around the home. Its basic formula consists of a pigment (derived from either synthetic or naturally occurring materials) suspended in a clear oil, water or synthetic polymer-based medium – which acts as the vehicle for the application and binding of the pigment to the underlying surface.

The two basic types of paint used in interior decoration – oil-based and water-based – are produced in a wide range of colours by the leading paint companies, and you should have little difficulty in obtaining either proprietary brands or the materials for mixing your own, from DIY retailers and specialist artists' suppliers. But as with most things, you get what you pay for. So, always buy the best quality paints you can afford.

Oil-Based Paints

PRIMERS: Solvent in white spirit (mineral spirits) and usually white or pink in colour, they are available in different formulations for sealing bare plaster, wood and metal prior to undercoating.

UNDERCOAT: A dense matt finish paint – usually white, but available in a limited number of other colours. It is applied in one or two coats over previously primed or decorated surfaces, to provide a ready-keyed, opaque surface suitable for flat-oil or eggshell ground coats. When mixing large quantities of glaze (see opposite), it can be used as a more economical substitute for white artists' oil.

FLAT-OIL: A high quality, matt finish paint. Available in white (from specialist decorators' and artists' suppliers), it can be tinted with artists' oils to a desired colour, and used over primed and undercoated surfaces to provide an opaque ground coat for most of the Fantasy Finishes outlined in this book. However, its matt finish makes it more absorbent, less hard-wearing, and therefore less suitable, for this purpose than the tougher, mid-sheen finish provided by eggshell (see below).

EGGSHELL: An opaque, mid-sheen finish paint, available in white and a wide range of colours (including fluorescent), it provides the most suitable ground coat for translucent oil- or water-based glazes. It can be tinted with artists' oils to obtain the desired colour, and rubbed down with wet and dry paper to produce a smooth, non-porous surface. Moreover, it can provide an economical, hard-wearing and effective substitute for artists' oils when mixing and tinting oil-based glazes (see *Mixing Glazes*, opposite).

METALLIC PAINTS: Thick opaque paints available in a number of vibrant colours, the most common being silver and gold. They are used in fairly small quantities (the exception being for Metal Patina effects, pages 96-7) in a number of the Fantasy Finishes.

ARTISTS' OILS: These are available from specialist decorators' and artists' suppliers in a wide range of makes and colours – as usual, buy the best you can afford. They can be used to tint opaque undercoats, flat-oils and eggshells to the required colour: and combined with a clear medium – consisting of scumble, linseed oil and white spirit in varying proportions – to produce the vibrant, translucent coloured glazes used in most of the Fantasy Finishes (see pages 96-123). However, unlike thinned eggshell glazes, they normally need to be protected with one or two coats of varnish (see *Varnishes*, page 89).

Mixing various artists' oils together allows you to create your own custom colours; this can be very useful if you are trying to decorate walls to match the colour of fabrics elsewhere in a room, but are unable to find the right ready-mixed retail paint.

Water-based Paints

EMULSIONS: Sometimes known as latex paints, they are widely available in a variety of colours and opaque matt and mid-sheen (silk) finishes. They can be thinned with water and clear emulsion glaze (water-based varnish, see page 89) to produce translucent glazes and washes, and tinted with artists' acrylics to produce custom colours.

Unfortunately, they have a number of shortcomings when used in decorative paint techniques. Firstly, if used as an opaque ground coat they have a rougher finish (unsuitable for rubbing down with wet-and-dry paper), which is much more porous than oil-based eggshell. This makes any superimposed glazes start drying too quickly to be properly 'worked' over the surface. Secondly, a similar problem arises if they are thinned with water to make translucent tinted glazes (see *Mixing Glazes*, opposite). They dry very quickly, again allowing insufficient time to 'work' the paint. However, this is not a problem with some Fantasy Finishes (see Plaster, pages 104-5) and Two-colour Distressing, pages 112-3). And thirdly, they will induce rust if applied directly to bare metal, and may raise the grain if brushed over bare wood.

ARTISTS' GOUACHE: Available from artists' suppliers, these high quality water-based pigments can be used to tint emulsion glazes to the required colours – which have an ethereal, brushy quality when applied over an opaque ground. However, for a tougher, more resilient finish, it is recommended that you use artists' acrylics for tinting emulsion paints and glazes.

ARTISTS' ACRYLICS: These water-based paints are available from artists' suppliers in a wide variety of colours. They can be applied neat with a brush or a palette knife to simulate the impasto of an oil painting, or thinned to produce translucent glazes in their own right. But, their fast drying times, while allowing you to produce rapid overlays of colour, and making them suitable for painting fabrics, have all the attendant disadvantages of emulsions. Consequently, they are most useful for tinting white and pale emulsion glazes to the required colour (see *Mixing Glazes*, below right and overleaf).

FABRIC PAINTS
Available in a wide range of colours and for a variety of fabrics, they can be diluted in water and mixed together to produce other colours. They come in pearlised, transparent, opaque and fluorescent finishes. You should always follow carefully the manufacturer's instructions regarding mixing, stability, permanence, drying times and cleaning.

ADDITIONAL MATERIALS
JAPAN GOLD SIZE: A quick-drying varnish used as an adhesive for gold or metal leaf.

TRANSFER METAL LEAF: Available in gold or silver, or cheaper Dutch metal alloy or aluminium substitutes, transfer leaf can be applied over gold size on large or small, and flat or moulded surfaces. (See Lapis Lazuli, pages 98-9.)

Fabric paints are widely available in many colours from craft shops and artists' suppliers.

GLAZES
For our purposes a tinted glaze is a paint (pigment suspended in a clear medium) which has been sufficiently thinned in a solvent clear medium to make it semi-transparent when applied over an opaque, white or coloured ground coat. The transparency or translucency of the tinted glaze (or glazes) allows the underlying ground colour to 'ghost' through, producing subtle gradations and combinations of colours over the decorated surface, and creating a sense of depth in the finish – effects that are at the heart of the decorative paint techniques shown in this book.

WATER-BASED GLAZES These consist of proprietary matt or mid-sheen emulsion paint (or white emulsion tinted with artists' acrylics or gouache), that has been substantially thinned with water or emulsion glaze (see *Water-based varnish*, page 89) to produce a translucent coloured glaze. They have a thinner, less rich, and more brushy appearance than oil-based glazes, and their very fast drying times make them less 'workable', and therefore suitable for only a few of the Fantasy Finishes (see Plaster, pages 104-5 and Two-colour Distressing, pages 112-3).

OIL-BASED GLAZES These consist of varying proportions of scumble, linseed oil and white spirit, which combine to make a colourless, transparent medium that is tinted with artists' oils (or eggshell paints) to produce the high quality, translucent coloured glazes used in most of the finishes on pages 96-123.

The scumble glaze is available from artists' suppliers as a white or honey-coloured transparent liquid. Thinned with white spirit it becomes colourless when brushed out over a surface. Linseed oil is a pale yellow, viscous liquid that is an ingredient both of the scumble glaze and the clear medium. It is available in decolourised, refined form from artists' suppliers. And white spirit or denatured alcohol is a clear liquid used as a solvent and thinning agent in the clear medium. Available from DIY outlets and specialist decorators' and artists' suppliers, it is also used for removing oil-based paints, glazes and varnishes from brushes.

Mixing glazes
Whether oil or water-based, glazes can be mixed to create an almost infinite range of colours, and adjusted to varying degrees of translucency, simply by following the simple method outlined below.

In each of the finishes illustrated on pages 98-123 the colours and proportions have been specified to produce 1 litre (¼ U.S. gal) of glaze. However, if you require only a half litre of glaze to cover the surface, simply halve the quantities of the pigments and clear medium accordingly. And correspondingly, if you need 2 litres double the quantities.

Over and above mixing the tinted glazes specified for the Fantasy Finishes on pages 98-123, you are encouraged to experiment with colour, and make up your own glazes (again using the mixing technique outlined below). Though before you start it is recommended that you refer to pages 90-3 for guidance on the various properties of colours, and the effects that can be produced by mixing them together and applying them over different grounds.

Finally, always adopt a systematic approach to mixing glazes. And keep a note of the names and quantities of the colours, and the proportions of the clear medium. This will allow you to replicate the glaze, if required, at a future date.

MIXING OIL-BASED GLAZES: Please note that in a number of the glazes specified in the Fantasy Finishes step-by-steps (see pages 98-123), the proportions of the clear medium – scumble, linseed and white spirit – vary. This is because each finish requires glazes that will 'behave' in specific ways and produce different effects.

Broadly speaking, a higher proportion of scumble glaze in the clear medium will result in a softer textured, slower drying glaze which retains the 'print' of the applicator you are using (such as a textured sponge or a flogger). Using more linseed oil will create a smoother textured glaze, again with a slower drying time – this is particularly useful if it has to be extensively 'worked' over the surface to achieve the desired effect. Increasing the percentage of white spirit will give the glaze a thinner, 'grittier' texture and speed up drying time. However, the great advantage of white spirit is that, unlike scumble or linseed, it causes little or no discoloration and darkening of the glaze when applied over surfaces exposed to low levels of light (such as long corridors and hallways). For each Fantasy Finish it is recommended that, initially, you mix every glaze to the specified proportions of scumble, linseed and white spirit. Then, if you feel the glaze needs minor changes when it is applied over a particular surface, don't be afraid to make adjustments (see step 5 below).

You will need up to five bowls or containers (A,B,C,D, and E) for mixing a glaze. Each should have a minimum capacity of 1 litre (¼ U.S. gal) preferably 2.
1 Prepare the clear medium in container A: pour in the neat scumble glaze; slowly add linseed oil, mixing it into the scumble with an old fitch; and finally add white spirit, making sure all three ingredients are thoroughly blended together.
2 Pour some of the clear medium into container B – to a depth of approximately 1 cm (½ in).
3 Slowly blend the coloured pigments (paints or artists' oils) one at a time into the clear medium in container B, either until you have added the specified quantities of each, or achieved roughly the required colour if you are making up your own glaze. Use an old fitch, and make sure all the pigments are broken down and evenly dispersed, so that the mixture becomes a creamy liquid paste.
4 Check the paste against the colour swatches relating to the relevant Fantasy Finish – remember, at this stage you are trying to match up the colour, and not the transparency, of the glaze. If you are satisfied with the colour match, proceed straight to step 6.
5 If the colour is nearly right and just needs some minor adjustments, pour a third of the creamy liquid paste from container B into container C and add a spot of this or a touch of that . . . until you are satisfied.

On the other hand if the colour is not at all what you had in mind, repeat steps 2 and 3 in container C adjusting the proportions of the colours accordingly.
6 Gradually blend the creamy coloured liquid from container C (or from container B, if the mix was right at stage 4) back into the clear medium in container A. Keep stopping to test the glaze on the surface to be decorated, or a piece of eggshelled card. Once you have reached the required degree of transparency in the glaze, stop adding colour and proceed to step 9.
7 If you find you have blended all the colour into the clear medium in container A, and the resulting glaze is too translucent when brushed out over the surface, pour a little of it into container D (approximately 1 cm/ half an inch deep), and slowly blend in more pigments (paints or artists' oils) in the same proportions as they were added in step 3.
8 Gradually blend the creamy coloured liquid from container D back into container A. As in step 6, keep stopping to test the glaze over the surface, and cease adding once you have achieved the required degree of transparency/opacity in the glaze.
9 Now strain the correctly mixed glaze in container A through a filter into container E, after which it is ready for application.

MIXING WATER-BASED GLAZES: Employ the same method, as outlined above, for mixing oil-based glazes. However, substitute water and water-based matt glaze for scumble, linseed oil and white spirit, and emulsions and acrylics for artists' oils and eggshell paints. (See Plaster, pages 104-5, and Two-Colour Distressing, pages 112-3, for examples of water-based glazes.)

Varnishes and varnishing

Most of the Fantasy Finishes, unless otherwise specified, should be protected against scuffing, general wear and tear, water and condensation. This involves the application of one or more coats of varnish, and there are a number of different types available. Each has advantages and disadvantages relating to durability and discoloration, as described below, and which one you choose is to some degree a matter of compromise. However, to ensure the best results there are a few basic rules you should always follow:

1 Make sure the surface to be varnished is completely dry, and free from dust and debris.

2 The surrounding area should be as dust-free as possible, and all draughts should be eliminated to avoid dust being blown in from other areas and to stop the varnish drying out as you apply it.

3 Avoid wearing clothing that sheds fibres.

4 Use a fine-bristled varnishing brush (which should never be used for anything else) and keep a wet edge going as you cover a surface.

5 Try to work in a warm, dry atmosphere – damp, draughty surroundings can give some varnishes a milky white 'bloom' as they dry.

6 Always follow the manufacturer's instructions in relation to stirring, thinning and drying times.

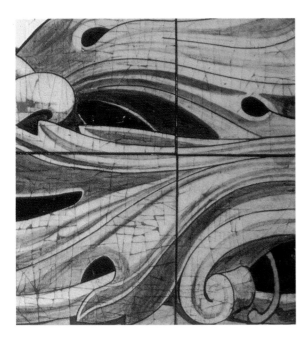

Above: *The surface of these hand-painted fake wall tiles has been crazed and 'aged' using a Crackle varnish. Because they are in a bathroom, the finish has been protected with a clear oil-based varnish.*

OIL-BASED VARNISHES: These traditional varnishes are available from artists' and specialist decorators' suppliers in matt, mid-sheen and gloss finishes. They tend to enrich any colours they are brushed over, and their fairly slow drying times make them susceptible to picking up any dust from the atmosphere. While offering solid protection against wear and tear and condensation, they tend to yellow with age (especially in poorly lit areas). However, thinning them with up to 10 percent white spirit speeds up drying times, and thus helps to reduce this problem.

POLYURETHANE VARNISHES: Widely available in matt, mid-sheen (satin) and gloss finishes, these modern, easy-to-apply varnishes offer a high degree of protection against scuffing, normal wear and tear, heat, alcohol, water and condensation. While this makes them very effective in bathrooms and kitchens, and on table tops, they tend to enrich the colours they are applied over, and have a reputation for yellowing with age (again especially in poorly lit areas), although recently manufacturers have begun to overcome this.

YACHT VARNISH: Available from DIY outlets and specialist suppliers, this clear gloss finish varnish provides durable protection for painted floors (though you may require up to five coats). Unfortunately it yellows and darkens any finish, a process that intensifies with age.

WATER-BASED VARNISHES: Emulsion glazes are available from specialist decorators' suppliers in matt, mid-sheen and gloss finishes. They can be applied over water and oil-based glazes (over the latter only in accordance with the manufacturer's instructions). They are a milky white colour, but when brushed out they dry to a transparent finish which hardly discolours or yellows with age (even in poorly lit areas). This, together with a fast drying time, which minimizes the risk of picking up dust, makes them ideal for protecting the subtle appearance of many Fantasy Finishes – especially when pastel colours have been used. However, they do not offer the same degree of protection against water, condensation and general wear and tear as polyurethane and oil-based types, so their use will partly depend on the finishes' location.

CRACKLE VARNISH: Water- and oil-based varnishes specifically formulated for achieving a crackle finish. They are available from specialist decorators' suppliers.

The use of colour

The success or otherwise of most decorative paint schemes is largely dependent on an appropriate use of colour. Colours can be combined to good or bad effect, and may be spectacularly impressive in one setting and an eyesore in another. This section provides you with a brief introduction to the basic qualities of colour and, while recognising that visual responses to colour are highly individual, offers a few related guidelines on how to set about choosing and mixing colours to create different sorts of effects.

The dimensions of colour
Colour can be said to have three basic characteristics:

HUE describes whether a colour is red or green or yellow or blue etc, and thus allows us to distinguish one colour from another.

CHROMATIC INTENSITY is a measurement of the strength of a colour, and relates to its saturation – if you like, how concentrated or pure it is, and to what degree it has been tainted or dulled by black, white or other colours.

THE BASIC PALETTE

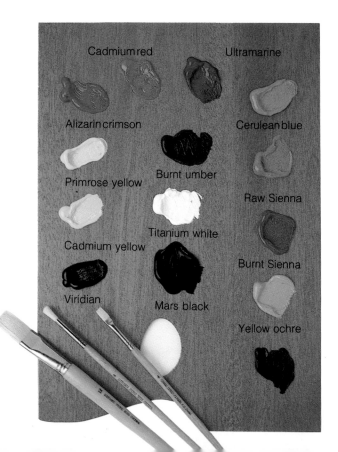

Cadmium red

Ultramarine

Alizarin crimson

Cerulean blue

Primrose yellow

Burnt umber

Raw Sienna

Titanium white

Cadmium yellow

Burnt Sienna

Viridian

Mars black

Yellow ochre

TONAL VALUE is a measurement of a colour's luminosity. In other words, how much light it reflects or absorbs, and therefore how light or dark it appears.

Colours can be divided into three major categories:
PRIMARIES: Pure red, blue and yellow, from which, in theory, all other colours can be mixed.

SECONDARIES: Colours that are produced by mixing two primaries. For example, yellow + blue = green.

TERTIARIES: Colours that are produced by mixing primary and secondary colours together. Thus, for example, purple + green = olive.

And two sub-categories:
TINTS are produced by adding white to colours, thus making them lighter and raising their tonal value.

SHADES are produced by adding black to colours, making them darker and lowering their tonal value.

The painter's palette
In the sixteenth century the painter Titian declared that an artist needed only three basic hues on his palette: magenta, cyan and yellow. But trying to mix all colours down from these three primaries, plus black and white, would create difficulties for the decorative painter. As each new combination is mixed further away from the primaries it produces an ever increasing reduction in the chromatic intensity (saturation) and tonal value (luminosity) of the resulting colour(s). If this mixing process is taken too far, you can end up with a dirty, sludgy mess.

However, used with restraint, mixing from a limited palette does enable you to produce the more mellow, less vivid, colours such as powder blue or coral pink, so often used to good effect in decorative schemes. Consequently, if you wish to mix alternative colours to those specified for each of the Fantasy Finishes (see pages 96-123), you are advised to equip yourself with a basic palette of ready-mixed artists' oils or acrylics (see left), from which a full range of additional colours can be created. And, by mixing no more than three colours together at any one time, you will avoid too great a loss of chromatic intensity and tonal value. Once you begin to mix different colours, and brush or sponge them out over a surface, you will discover that certain combinations will make roughly equal demands on the eye. That is, no one colour will dominate, or be dominated by, the colours around it. This is because they all have, or have been mixed to, approximately the same chromatic intensity and tonal value. A good illustration of how this effect can be used is in the Tiffany finish on pages 118-9, where all four colours command roughly equal attention in the composition.

On the other hand, more saturated colours with a higher tonal value than those around them may 'advance' at the latters' expense. In other words they make a more vivid impression on the eye, and tend to dominate the other colours. You may wish to exploit this characteristic of colour to emphasise particular aspects of a composition. Alternatively, if you feel that one of your colours is too dominant, you can 'subdue it', or 'knock it back', by adding a little of another colour (mixing titanium white with a little burnt umber, for example), until its chromatic intensity and tonal value have been reduced to the level of the colours around it.

The colour wheel

Leonardo da Vinci's statement that 'colours appear what they are not, according to the ground which surrounds them', highlights the importance of taking

Pure colour

Tint

Shade

Above: *Various Metal Patina finishes (see pages 96-7) applied to test cards. It is always a good idea to first try out different finishes on card, and then place them in the room to be decorated, so that they can be assessed in situ.*

Left: *These coloured squares show the difference between a pure colour, a tint, and a shade.*

Tints are produced by adding white to a (pure) colour, thus making them lighter and raising their tonal value.

Shades are produced by adding black to a (pure) colour, thus making them darker and lowering their tonal value.

into account the fact that the appearance of one colour is always modified by the presence of another, whether it is all around it, adjacent to it, or ghosting through it from underneath (like an opaque ground through a translucent glaze, as in all of the Fantasy Finishes on pages 98-123). In other words, colours should not be viewed in isolation. For a better understanding of this, and of how to go about choosing ones that will work together in a decorative scheme, you should refer to the colour wheel below.

Complementary colours

Complementaries are opposite each other on the colour wheel. Thus the complementary of blue is yellow-red, and the complementary of red is blue-green. If complementaries are mixed together in equal proportions they neutralize each other and produce a gray colour. Whereas, if a small quantity of one is added to a larger quantity of another, it will soften and dull the latter without changing its tone.

But more importantly, complementary colours, when placed in close proximity to each other on a surface, will heighten each other's saturation, or chromatic intensity (a process known as irradiation). The degree to which they do this is partly dependent

on their respective chromatic intensities and tonal values in the first place. Indeed some complementaries, such as a vivid primary red and a saturated, luminous green, will irradiate each other to such an extent that most people would find them uncomfortable to look at. However, slightly less saturated and luminous complementaries (and near complementaries) can be used to create vibrant contrasts in a composition without appearing garish.

Discordant colours and off-hues

All colours, including the primaries, have a tonal relationship to each other. For example, pure yellow is lighter than pure red. However, this relationship changes as tints and shades of these hues are created – sometimes to the point where it can be said they do not work well together, such as pink (red plus white) and mustard (yellow plus black), for example. In this case they are termed discordant, and might be described as 'clashing'.

The problem of 'incompatibility' also occurs between off-hues. That is, colours with common characteristics, such as vivid pink and maroon, which are both derived from red but are not actually adjacent on the colour wheel. When used in close proximity they seem to

THE COLOUR WHEEL

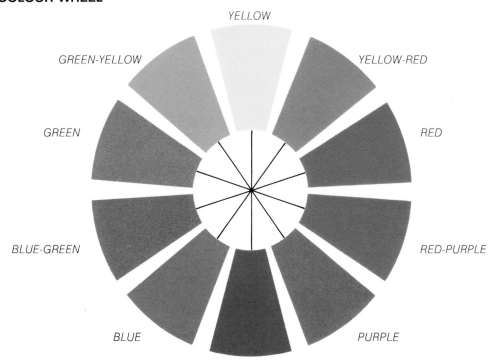

YELLOW

GREEN-YELLOW

YELLOW-RED

GREEN

RED

BLUE-GREEN

RED-PURPLE

BLUE

PURPLE

PURPLE-BLUE

diminish or detract from each other, again to the point of 'clashing'.

However, while there is no hard and fast rule restricting the use of discordants and off-hues in combination, the proportions in which they are employed in any decorative scheme have a considerable bearing on whether or not they prove compatible. For example, a thin section of moulding, such as a dado rail, can be picked out to good effect by using one of two discordant colours, while surrounding walls may be painted in the other, whereas adjacent walls painted in two discordant colours will almost invariably 'clash'.

Warm and cool colours

Another useful way of looking at colours is to categorize them in terms of how 'warm' or 'cool' they are. Broadly, colours that are closest to red and yellow on the colour wheel, are considered both 'warm' and 'advancing'. That is, they make surfaces appear closer and thus can be used to cheer up cold, poorly lit rooms. Moreover, lighter tints of these colours will make a room look brighter.

On the other hand, colours that are closest to blue and green on the colour wheel are considered 'cool' and 'retreating' (that is, they give surfaces depth, and take them further away). Thus, they can be used to make stuffy rooms feel cooler – lighter tints imparting a fresh, airy quality to a decorative scheme.

But once again, it is important to remember that the appearance, and our perception, of a colour is always modified by the presence of other colours. For example, duck egg blue is considered warm because it has red in it; while cerise (a red) is felt to be cool because it has blue in it. This characteristic enables you to make colours 'warmer' by mixing in a little of another colour that is closer to red on the colour wheel, and 'cooler' by adding a different colour that is nearer to blue. And it allows you to use translucent glazes to give either warm or cool casts to otherwise cool or warm underlying, opaque coloured grounds.

However, it is important to remember that complementary warm and cool colours, if placed in close proximity to each other (rather than mixed together), can irradiate each other to a certain extent. Thus, if you hold a bright, warm red rose up against an icy-blue wall, the chromatic intensity, luminosity and warmth of the rose will be enhanced by the chromatic intensity, luminosity and coolness of the wall, and *vice versa* – an effect you may wish to use or avoid in any scheme.

The emotional response to colour

Our response to the 'warmth' or 'coolness' of colour is essentially an emotional one. Indeed it is possible to further define colours with reference to how they influence thought and feeling. Thus, reds and yellows may be considered stimulating, greens calming and soothing, and blues and purples depressing. However, because our response to colour is often highly individual, such generalisations can be as misleading as they are useful. For example, some people don't find green soothing, or blue in the least depressing. In other words, if a particular colour, or hue, elicits a favourable response in you, don't be put off using it simply because a colour theorist stipulates your reaction should be something else altogether!

Colour and inspiration

To develop ideas on how to use colour in varying combinations you are encouraged to look at the examples of interiors shown throughout this book, as well as fine art, fabrics, interior design magazines, and nature itself. Learn to 'pull objects apart', resolving them into their constituent colours. You will discover that most things, from mushrooms to blocks of stone, are made up of a number of colours – pinks, grays, blues, black etc – each modifying the effect of the other and contributing to the overall appearance and colour of the whole. A recognition of this quality will be of tremendous assistance to you in devising alternative colours for many Fantasy Finishes, such as Porphyry (see pages 102-3) and Stone Blocking (see pages 100-1).

However, sources of inspiration should not be looked at in isolation. For example, if you feel the colours of a piece of fabric or pottery would be appropriate for the walls of a room, it is very important to look at these item(s) in the room itself. In this way you can discover the effect of the light (natural and artificial) on the colours. For example, a cold light may need a warm yellow or pink to offset it. Similarly, if you decide to mix your own opaque paints or translucent glazes to match or harmonize with existing fixtures and fittings (furniture, carpets and curtains etc), it is important to keep trying out swatches of the colours on the surfaces to be decorated (or on eggshelled card) in order to assess their compatibility *in situ*.

Finally, when choosing and mixing colours and finishes for a particular room, take into account its architectural features – good and bad (from elegant fire surrounds to ugly boxed-in pipes). As with most of the interiors shown throughout the book, judicious use of 'warm' or 'cool', 'advancing' or 'retreating', lighter or darker, complementary or discordant, saturated or unsaturated colour combinations will enable you to highlight attractive aspects, disguise uglier ones and 'visually adjust' the proportions of a room to meet your own aesthetic and decorative requirements.

chapter eight

techniques – the finishes

IN THE FOLLOWING PAGES YOU ARE SHOWN
how to create fourteen different Fantasy Finishes.
In each example, easy to follow step-by-step
instructions and illustrations, and specified
glazes and accompanying colour swatches, will
enable you to reproduce these impressive
decorative effects on all manner of surfaces
around your home. Furthermore, you are
encouraged to make colour and compositional
adjustments to the various finishes to meet your
own decorative requirements, and to this end
suggested colour and pattern variations are
shown at the end of most sections.

Metal patina — Verdigris

The verdigris finish illustrated here is but one of a number of metal patina effects — colour and compositional variations are shown at the end of the step-by-step instructions — that can be created with proprietary eggshell paints, brushed out straight from the tin. The technique employed is both simple and versatile — you could, for example, stop at the end of step 4 if you require a striking bronze/copper effect — and the finish is hardwearing (it doesn't require varnishing), which makes it suitable for decorating large or small areas, including raised mouldings, anywhere in the home.

GLAZES

A Slate gray eggshell paint – unthinned.

B Bronze-gold metallic paint – unthinned.

C Mid-green eggshell paint – unthinned.

D Light green eggshell paint – unthinned.

1 Apply a minimum of two coats of red oxide eggshell paint over the previously prepared surface (see pages 74-6), to establish an unbroken expanse of opaque colour. Use a smooth pile roller, rather than a standard decorators' brush, to create a lightly stippled texture over the surface, and preferably rub down each coat after it has dried (approximately 24 hours) with wet and dry paper.
2 Apply a slate gray eggshell paint (A) – shown left – straight from the tin, using a dry, standard decorators' brush. Put it on sparingly and brush it out thoroughly, both vertically and horizontally (avoid diagonal sweeps), allowing the red ground coat to ghost through in patches. Then leave to dry for 24 hours.

1

2

3

4

5

6

3 Now apply a bronze-gold metallic paint (B) − shown left − straight from the tin. As in step 2, the object is to apply it sparingly, brush it out thoroughly, and slowly build up a broken finish that allows the underlying slate gray and red oxide ground to ghost through in patches.
4 While the bronze-gold coat is still wet, rub it down with a dry, lint-free cotton rag (or one moistened with a little white spirit if the surface has nearly dried). The object is both to re-distribute and cut back the bronze-gold in places, thereby varying the density of colour across the surface, and giving greater definition to those patches where the ground coats are more prominent.

Which areas you concentrate on and the amount of pressure you use when rubbing are largely a matter of composition − but use the illustration for guidance, avoid diagonal sweeps, and don't overdo the white spirit, or you will smear the paint. Then allow the surface to dry for approximately 24 hours.
5 Apply a mid-green eggshell paint (C) − shown left − straight from the tin. Brush it out both lightly and thoroughly, up and down and from side to side, once again allowing the underlying ground to ghost through in random patches.

While the paint is still wet (ie, almost immediately) use a dry, lint-free cotton rag to rub down and wipe out any build-up of colour in those areas where you feel more of the contrasting ground should show through.
6 As the mid-green eggshell is drying, sparingly apply a lighter green eggshell paint (D) − shown left − straight from the tin. Once again, use a dry brush to gradually build up a broken finish that allows the combination of underlying ground coats to subtly ghost through.

In this example, the lighter green paint has not been applied to the skirting, thereby creating a contrast with the lighter wall above.

When the surface has dried thoroughly it can, if desired, be waxed and polished to enrich and slightly darken the colours.

VARIATIONS

Variation A is a Lead finish created by using the same technique as for Verdigris. Two tones of gray eggshell and silver metallic paint were brushed out over a black eggshell ground, and 'smeared' in places, with the rag, to adjust the composition. **Variation B** is a pastiche metal patina effect simply achieved by following steps 1-4, and applying orange-gold metallic and red eggshell paints over a light-red ground. **Variation C** is a simulation of corroded metal, created by the application of brown eggshell and aluminium paints over a reddy-brown ground.

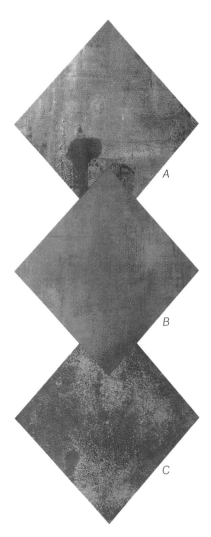

A

B

C

Lapis lazuli

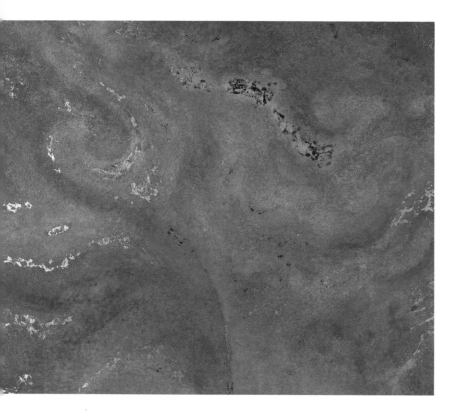

The finish illustrated here is a fantasy simulation of the ultramarine blue and gold-veined natural gemstone. Its striking appearance is best confined to smaller areas such as wall panels, and decorative items like jewellery boxes. If you do intend to apply it over a larger area, only work on a couple of square yards or metres at a time, and refer to page 76 for advice on blending adjacent sections together. Successful results depend on a good ground coat, assessing the composition of the finish before and during application and adjusting the sense of depth and swirling movement accordingly, and applying metal leaf with discretion.

GLAZES

A 100ml Prussian blue and 5ml white artists' oils per litre of 30% scumble, 25% linseed oil and 45% white spirit.

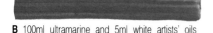

B 100ml ultramarine and 5ml white artists' oils per litre of medium as in (A) above.

1 Apply a minimum of two coats of a very pale blue eggshell paint over the previously prepared surface (see pages 74-6), to establish an unbroken expanse of opaque colour. Preferably use a smooth pile roller rather than a standard decorators' brush, and rub down each coat after it has dried (approximately 24 hours) with wet and dry paper.

2 Mix up a mid-blue glaze (A) and a darker blue glaze (B), as shown left. (And see pages 87-8 on mixing glazes.) Using a textured decorators' sponge (see page 81), dab glaze (A) onto the surface to build up cloudy gradations of translucent colour, through which the paler ground coat ghosts through.

1

2

3

4

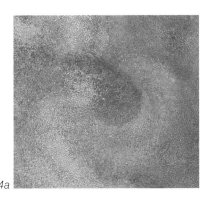

4a

5

3 While the surface is still wet, moisten a lint-free cotton rag with a little white spirit and wipe it through the glaze to reveal the ground coat and create the distinctive swirls of lapis. Keep turning the rag so that you remove glaze, rather than smear it back on.

The shape and position of the swirls is largely a matter of personal preference, but use the illustration for reference and try to create a sense of movement over the surface.

4 Again while the glaze is still wet, moisten a textured sponge with a little white spirit and gently dab it over the surface to soften and blend the swirls into the background. Then allow the glaze to dry for approximately 24 hours.

4a This detail illustrates the cloudy swirling shapes, the subtle gradations of colour and the sense of depth that can be created by softening and blending with the textured sponge.

5 Using a clean sponge, dab and stipple the darker blue glaze (B) into some of the lighter channels to form cloudy, broken patches that accentuate the swirling curves of the finish.

Once again the size, shape and position of the darker blue patches is largely a matter of personal preference, but use the illustration for guidance.

6 While the glaze is still wet, soften and blend the darker blue patches into the background, using a badger softener – gently sweeping the bristles along the curves to emphasise, once again, the sense of swirling movement in the finish. Then allow the surface to dry.

7 Using a small artists' brush, apply a thin film of goldsize (available from artists' suppliers) along various curves that you wish to highlight. Again, this is a matter of composition, but use the illustration for reference.

Then place a sheet of gold leaf or Dutch metal (available from artists' suppliers) over the patches of wet goldsize, and rub over the back of the sheet with your finger or the handle of a brush. Carefully peel

6

7

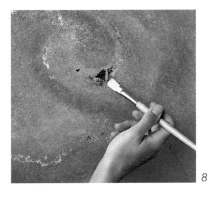

8

back the sheet, to leave the gold leaf stuck to the goldsize.

8 Gently break up the leaf with the dry bristles of an artists' brush, removing much of it and leaving broken pieces behind on the surface.

Allow the finish to dry thoroughly, and then apply one coat of a mid-sheen, oil-based varnish for protection (see page 89).

Stone blocking

The stone block effect can be used to lend an air of monumental solidity to otherwise featureless plaster walls. And by carrying it over fixtures such as skirtings, doors and architrave, it is possible to emphasise the sculptural and architectural qualities of structure and form in a room. To this end you are encouraged to study the construction of buildings where real stone has been used, and to look closely at the stone itself. Finally, in a painted fantasy finish, successful results depend on gradually building up the subtle colours and texture of the stone blocks and, as no natural stone is identical, avoiding uniformity across the surface.

GLAZES

A 60ml white, 25ml Oxford ochre and 3ml black artists' oils per litre of 35% scumble, 20% linseed oil and 45% white spirit.

B 60ml white, 25ml raw Sienna and 3ml black artists' oils per litre of medium as in (A) above.

C Glaze (A) tinted with a little ultramarine and burnt Sienna artists' oils.

D Glaze (A) tinted with a little burnt Sienna artists' oil.

E Glaze (A) tinted with a little white and black artists' oils.

1 Apply a minimum of two coats of a pale ivory eggshell paint over the previously prepared surface (see pages 74-6), to establish an unbroken expanse of opaque colour. Preferably use a smooth pile roller, rather than a standard decorators' brush, and lightly rub down each coat after it has dried (approximately 24 hours) with wet and dry paper.

It is important to note that whatever colour you use for the ground coat will be the colour of the groutlines between the stone blocks in the finished wall.

2 Using a spirit level, a ruler, a set-square and a water-based crayon, lightly draw the outlines of the stone blocks. Make the blocks along the skirting (and on any architrave or dado rails) twice as long as those on the wall.

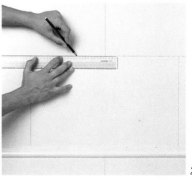

1

2

3

4

5

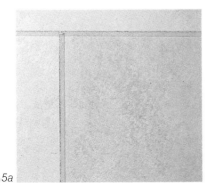

5a

6

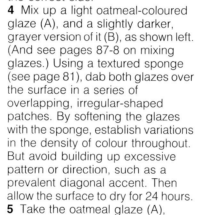

7

3 Using 5mm low-tack masking tape, mask off each block from those around it.

It is important to locate the predominant light source – in this case, off top left – and always position the tape so that on every vertical it butts up to the right-hand side of the outline, and on every horizontal it butts up to the bottom of the line (ie, the sides that are furthest from the light source). By doing this you will ensure that when the tape is removed the 'shadows' cast by the seemingly recessed groutlines (ie, the crayon lines) will always fall on the correct side.

4 Mix up a light oatmeal-coloured glaze (A), and a slightly darker, grayer version of it (B), as shown left. (And see pages 87-8 on mixing glazes.) Using a textured sponge (see page 81), dab both glazes over the surface in a series of overlapping, irregular-shaped patches. By softening the glazes with the sponge, establish variations in the density of colour throughout. But avoid building up excessive pattern or direction, such as a prevalent diagonal accent. Then allow the surface to dry for 24 hours.

5 Take the oatmeal glaze (A), separate it into 3 bowls, and tint each one to make (C) redder/warmer, (D) blue/colder, and (E) grayer/blacker, as shown left. (And see pages 87-8 on mixing glazes.) In other words, make up the sorts of colours that you see in natural stone.

Then, working on one block at a time, and holding a card along the edge you are working towards to protect the surrounding blocks, dab on each glaze in turn, with a sponge. The object, as in step 4, is to build up overlapping patches of broken, translucent colour.

5a Note the subtle gradations of colour gradually built up from the three glazes during step 5, and the absence of any noticeable pattern or accent across the surface.

6 When you have finished all the blocks, and the surface is dry, peel off the low-tack masking tape. Never rip the tape off the wall, or you might remove some of the ground coat!

7 Rub out the crayon outlines where they overlap at intersections. And, if any glaze has crept under the masking tape, touch up the grout lines with a small artists' brush and a little of the coloured eggshell ground coat used in step 1.

When the surface has dried thoroughly, apply two coats of a matt finish, clear water-based varnish for protection (see page 89).

Porphyry

The porphyry finish illustrated here is a pastiche of the hard variegated rock used in sculpture and as a decorative building material. As such, it can be applied to most surfaces around the home, but looks particularly effective on table tops and in wall panels. Predominantly purple and white in colour, the natural material consists of large crystals in a fine-grained ground-mass. However, to produce a fantasy finish you can employ any number of complementary colours, provided you simulate the essential structure and texture of the polished rock (see the variations opposite). Finally, when working over larger areas, refer to page 76 for advice.

GLAZES

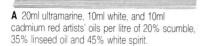

A 20ml ultramarine, 10ml white, and 10ml cadmium red artists' oils per litre of 20% scumble, 35% linseed oil and 45% white spirit.

B 40ml French blue, 30ml black, 30ml viridian and 10ml white artists' oils per litre of 25% scumble, 30% linseed oil and 45% white spirit.

C 130ml crimson, 10ml white and 10ml black artists' oils per litre of medium as in (B) above.

1 Apply a minimum of two coats of a pale stone eggshell paint over the previously prepared surface (see pages 74-6), to establish an unbroken expanse of opaque colour. Use either a smooth pile roller or a standard decorators' brush, and rub down each coat after it has dried (approximately 24 hours) with wet and dry paper.
2 Mix up a pale brown glaze (A), and an ink-blue glaze (B), as shown left. (And see pages 87-8 on mixing glazes.) Using a textured sponge (see page 81), apply glaze (A) over the ground coat. Employ a dabbing and stippling action to create cloudy gradations of colour across the surface.

1

2

3

4

5

6

3 While glaze (A) is still wet, use a clean sponge to dab randomly spaced, irregular-shaped patches of the inky blue glaze (B) over the surface. Gradually build up the colour, softening it as you go, to create a mottled finish with the underlying pale mauve/brown glaze ghosting through.

4 As the glazes are drying, charge an angled fitch with a clear medium of 75 percent white spirit and 25 percent scumble glaze, hold the brush some 5-6 ins (12-15 cms) from the surface, and pull your finger through the bristles to send a fine spray or spatter of the medium over the glaze. Repeat this process at intervals across the surface, then allow the glazes to dry for approximately 24 hours.

The white spirit in the medium will 'ciss', or open up, the glaze, to form small, circular patches in which the pigment is driven outwards from the centre (which thus becomes more translucent) to re-form into more opaque bands of colour around the perimeter. And the scumble glaze is added to the medium to stop the white spirit simply running down a vertical surface, thereby spoiling the effect.

N.B. Because this technique is quite difficult to control, it is strongly recommended that you practice first on a spare piece of paper pinned to a wall.

5 Mix up a rich red glaze (C), as shown left. (And see pages 87-8 on mixing glazes.) Dip the tip of a lint-free cotton rag into the glaze, remove any excess on a spare piece of paper, and lightly dab it over the surface to form small, broken patches of colour. The amount you apply is largely a matter of composition, but don't overdo it, and use the illustration for guidance.

6 While it is still wet, dab the surface with a square stippler to soften and blend the red glaze further into the background.

Allow the surface to dry thoroughly before adding one or two coats of matt finish, clear water- or oil-based varnish for protection (see page 89).

VARIATIONS

Variation A was created as in steps 1-7, and by applying gray and yellow glazes over an off-white ground. The composition was given a sharper definition by reducing the amount of softening and blending in step 6. **Variation B** was achieved by applying white and blue-black glazes over a pale blue ground. However, step 4 (cissing) was restricted to a very fine spray, and instead of softening and blending (step 6), the dried surface was rubbed down with wet and dry paper. **Variation C** was created by applying beige, gray and white metallic glazes over a gold ground, and steps 1-7 were followed.

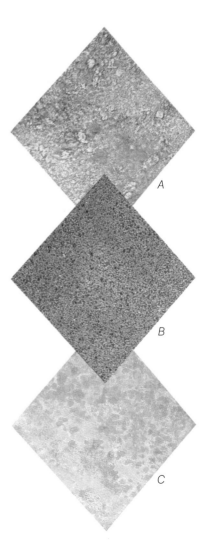

A

B

C

Plaster

This versatile effect can provide an understated and elegant finish on walls and ceilings in any room in the home. The simple technique enables one person to cover large areas quite quickly, and successful results can be achieved even over patchy, uneven surfaces. Glazes can be adjusted to make the composition lighter or darker, and relief mouldings, such as covings and picture rails, can be incorporated into the effect for a more integrated look. Here, a simple *trompe l'oeil* recessed panel has been included to demonstrate how large, featureless expanses of wall can be broken up into smaller, more interesting sections.

GLAZES

A Per litre: 25% white matt emulsion, 15% orange ochre acrylic, 30% matt glaze and 30% water.

B Per litre: 35% white matt emulsion, 5% red ochre and 5% black acrylic, 20% matt glaze and 35% water.

C Per litre: 40% white matt emulsion, 20% matt glaze and 40% water.

1 Apply a minimum of two coats of a very pale, beige emulsion paint over the previously prepared surface (see pages 74-6), using a standard decorators' brush or a medium pile roller. Don't worry if the ground coat is a bit patchy, or reveals a few brushmarks, as this will enhance the plaster finish. Then allow to dry thoroughly.

2 Mix up a pale, yellowy-brown glaze (A) as shown left. (And see pages 87-8 on mixing glazes.) Charge a textured sponge (see page 81) with the glaze, wiping any excess off on a spare piece of lining paper, and apply it over the surface. Use a gentle scrubbing action, working in all directions, to gradually build up subtle gradations of colour over the pale ground. And make a point of pushing the sponge into the recesses of any mouldings to ensure that they are covered. Then allow the surface to dry for approximately 4 or 5 hours.

1

2

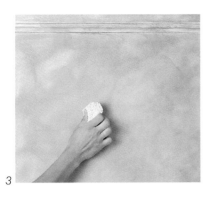

3

4

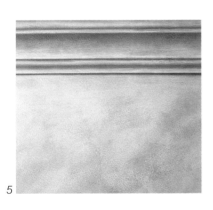

5

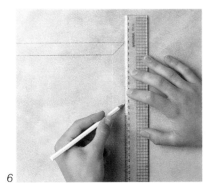

6

3 Mix up a slightly darker, grayer version (B) of the first glaze, as shown left. (And see pages 87-8 on mixing glazes.)

Again using a textured sponge, apply the glaze very sparingly over the surface (don't overload the sponge). Scrub quite firmly in all directions to build up a cloudy cover that allows the underlying glaze to ghost through in patches.

Keep standing back from the work to assess the overall composition, adding more of glaze (B) where you feel it should be made darker, and rubbing off the glaze with a clean sponge where you feel it should be lighter. Then allow the surface to dry for approximately 4 or 5 hours.

4 Mix up a translucent white glaze (C), as shown left. (And see pages 87-8 on mixing glazes.) Then scrub it over the surface with a sponge, using the same method as in steps 2 and 3. The white glaze will soften and tone down the underlying colour; and the application can be repeated if you wish to make the finish even lighter.

5 If desired, the finished surface, after it has dried thoroughly, can be protected with one coat of a matt finish, clear oil-based varnish – though this isn't strictly necessary.

6 If you are working on a large, unbroken expanse of wall, you can divide the surface into sections, using simple, *trompe l'oeil* panelling. (However, this must be done *before* varnishing, as described in step 5.)

Having established the location of the predominant light source – in this case, off top left – draw the outlines of the recessed panel, using the illustration for guidance. The sides of the recess that will be in shadow – here, the top and left (latter not shown) – should be outlined in pencil; while the sides that will reflect the predominant light source – here, right and bottom (latter not shown) – should be outlined in white crayon.

7 Mix up a dark, opaque, water-based glaze that matches the colour of the shadows cast by the cornice above (or the point where the wall meets the ceiling) – the closer the

7

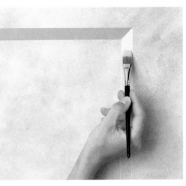

8

match, the more effective the finished *trompe l'oeil* will be.

Using an artists' brush, fill in the outlines of the top and left-hand edges of the recess.

8 Mix up an off-white, opaque water-based glaze and fill in the right-hand and bottom sides of the frame, again using an artists' brush and taking care to make a neat join in the corners.

Note how the finished frame (opposite) takes on a convincing three-dimensional appearance – a *trompe l'oeil*.

Watered silk

A watered silk finish looks especially effective when framed in a panel, simulating the centuries-old practice of lining the doors of wardrobes and bookcases with real silk. However, the technique outlined below can be applied over entire walls with equal success (use two people, and work on no more than a couple of square yards or metres at a time – refer to page 76 for advice). Obviously, different colours can be used (a variation is shown opposite), and watermarks and the texture of the fabric adjusted as required – billows and sags can be introduced by exaggerating the undulation of the brush during steps 6 and 7, for example.

GLAZES

A 200ml white undercoat, 10ml French blue, 1ml black, and 1ml primrose chrome artists' oils per litre of 25% scumble, 10% linseed oil and 65% white spirit.

B 200ml white undercoat, 15ml French blue, 1.5ml black, and 1.5ml primrose chrome per litre of medium as (A) above.

1 Apply a minimum of two coats of pale blue eggshell paint over the previously prepared surface (see pages 74-6), using either a smooth pile roller or a standard decorators' brush. Establish an unbroken expanse of opaque colour, and rub down each coat after it has dried (approximately 24 hours) with wet and dry paper.

2 Mix up a light blue glaze (A), as shown left. (And see pages 87-8 on mixing glazes.) Then brush it out evenly over the ground coat, using a standard decorators' brush, and finishing off in one direction – in this case vertically.

1

2

3 Dab and push the bristle tips of a dry glider brush sideways into the still wet glaze, to open it up and reveal vertical bands of ground coat, or 'watermarks'. Here, one irregular-shaped band has been cut out to run the full length of the centre of the panel, and randomly spaced shorter marks have been made on either side.

4 Moisten the bristles of a flogger with a little of the blue glaze (A), and gently drag the brush in a series of parallel vertical sweeps over the still wet surface, to soften the marks created in step 3 and generally accentuate the 'warp' of the 'fabric'. Then allow the surface to dry for approximately 24 hours.

. N.B. To avoid dragging glaze away from the top and bottom edges of the panel, where it meets the frame, the correct brush technique must be used: (a) lightly place the bristles of the flogger side-onto the surface, approximately ½ in (1.5 cm) from the edge of the top of the frame; (b) gently stipple the bristles forwards so that they just touch the frame; (c) lightly drag the bristles back across the surface in a continuous sweep, to just beyond the centre of the panel; (d) as you near the end of the stroke, gradually reduce pressure on the bristles and gently sweep the brush up and away from the surface; (e) now repeat this process starting directly opposite at the bottom of the frame. The point where any two brushstrokes meet in the middle of the panel is 'disguised' by the technique described in (d).

5 Mix up a slightly darker, translucent blue glaze (B), as shown left. (And see pages 87-8 on mixing glazes.) Brush it out vertically over glaze (A), using a standard decorators' brush. Don't worry if the application is a bit patchy, as this will enhance the finished composition.

6 Gently cross drag a glider brush moistened with white spirit through the wet glaze, to open it up and create the 'weft'. Use the brushstroke technique described in step 2, but introduce a slight undulation or wave into each sweep, and keep cleaning the brush on lint-free cotton rag.

7 Gently drag the bristle tips of a dry glider brush vertically down the surface, using a featherlight twisting and rocking action. The downward drag accentuates the warp, while the simultaneous side to side cutting action further opens up the weft of the fabric.

When the surface has dried, apply two coats of a clear, mid-sheen, water-based varnish for protection (see page 89).

VARIATION

This yellow Watered Silk variation was created using the same method employed in steps 1-8. However, in this case a number of parallel vertical bands, or 'watermarks', were made during step 3, and subsequent cross-dragging, in step 6, was used to adjust their prominence.

Antiquing

The various techniques used to antique, or distress, the watered silk panel left can be employed to artificially age virtually any painted finish. By simulating processes such as bleaching, scuffing, cracking, insect infestation, the accumulation of dirt and the build-up of patina, such techniques can be used discreetly to lend 'character' and faded elegance to otherwise pristine, featureless surfaces, or taken to extremes to create an exciting fantasy of delapidation and decay. However, do consider the sort of wear and tear any particular surface is likely to undergo — you wouldn't find woodworm in a stone block wall!

GLAZES

A Matt finish clear oil-based varnish tinted with a little white eggshell paint, and thinned with 10% white spirit.

B 50% black, 25% Oxford ochre, and 25% burnt Sienna artists' oils per litre of 85% scumble glaze and 15% white spirit.

1 Here, the watered silk panel created on pages 106-7 is used to demonstrate the 'ageing' process – the curved panel mouldings providing an ideal surface for this particular finish.
2 Having lightly rubbed down the surface to be decorated with wet and dry paper, use a fine bristled varnishing brush to apply a white tinted matt or mid-sheen varnish (A), as shown left. (And see pages 87-8 on mixing glazes.) Cover the moulding and the watered silk panel. Then allow the surface to dry for approximately 24 hours.
The object is to lighten the blue ground, and thus simulate the bleaching effects of long-term exposure to sunlight.

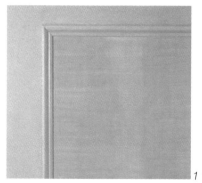

1

2

3 Rub down sections of the surface with medium-grade sandpaper to cut through the white varnish, remove patches of the blue watered silk finish, and thus reveal the paler blue ground coat underneath. The areas you concentrate on and the amount of pressure you apply are largely a matter of composition.

However, as the purpose of this step is to simulate fading and general wear and tear, make a point of rubbing back the colour along the raised sections of the mouldings – the area most vulnerable to scuffing and chaffing.

4 Mix up a brown tinted scumble glaze (B), as shown left. (And see pages 87-8 on mixing glazes.) Then brush it over the frame and panel, using the fine bristled varnishing brush. Don't worry if the coverage is a bit patchy, as you will be removing much of the glaze in the next step.

5 While the glaze is still wet, use a dry, lint-free cotton pad to wipe most of it off. Regularly turn the pad, so that you don't smear glaze back on, and rub up and down to leave uneven patches of translucent colour with the underlying ground coats ghosting through.

Again, for authenticity, remove most of the glaze from the convex surfaces of the mouldings, but leave some in the concave sections, where you would expect to see more shadow and to find a greater build-up of dust and dirt. Then allow the surface to dry for approx 24 hours.

6 Dip an artists' brush into the brown tinted glaze (B), hold it some 4-5 ins (10-15 cms) from the surface, and pull your finger through the bristles to spatter on, at random, fine droplets of glaze. The object is to simulate the ageing spots and holes often found on old fabric and wood.

N.B. It is a good idea to first try this technique on a spare piece of paper pinned to a wall, before starting in earnest. This will allow you to develop some control over the spatter, as well as discovering if you need to add a little clear scumble to glaze (B), to stop it running down the vertical surface and spoiling the effect.

7 A further option is to simulate more extensive 'damage' by moistening a lint-free cotton rag with cellulose thinners (available from auto accessory shops) and gently rubbing over sections of the surface. The thinners will etch through the layers of glaze, sometimes causing them to bubble and flake, and in places even cutting into the underlying primer!

However, be careful when you are doing this: wear protective goggles and rubber gloves, and open any windows and doors for ventilation.

8 After the surface has dried thoroughly, a final option is to polish it with a tinted wax to simulate a lustrous patina.

Crackle

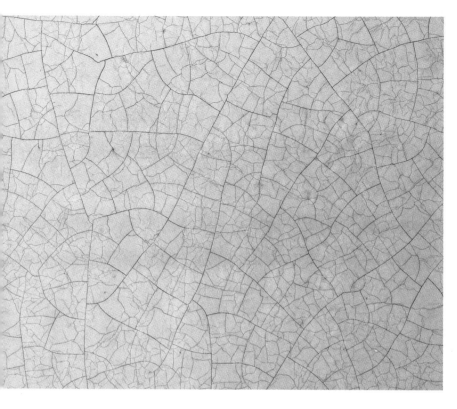

The finish illustrated below is a pastiche of the fine crazing often found in old varnished surfaces. As such, it looks particularly effective when used to decorate small items of furniture, simple ceramic ornaments and door and wall panels. However, it is not recommended for large areas, because it would be very difficult to lay off the rapidly drying crackle varnish without creating ugly brush or roller marks. By using different types of glazes – alternative colour and pattern variations are shown opposite – a striking variety of crackle finishes can be produced, though it is not always possible to predetermine the exact pattern and extent of the crazing.

GLAZE

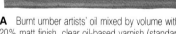

A Burnt umber artists' oil mixed by volume with 20% matt finish, clear oil-based varnish (standard, not crackle type).

1 Apply a minimum of two coats of an off-white eggshell ground coat over the previously prepared surface (see pages 74-6), to establish an unbroken expanse of opaque colour. Preferably use a smooth pile roller, rather than a standard decorators' brush, and rub down each coat after it has dried (approximately 24 hours) with wet and dry paper.

At the same time, apply the eggshell ground coat over an A4-sized piece of test card.

2 Using a smooth pile roller, apply a further unthinned coat of the off-white colour employed for the eggshell ground. Make sure that you don't leave any unsightly roller-texture marks in the paint, as these will be highlighted by the varnish applied in step 3.

At the same time, make the same application over the A4 test card.

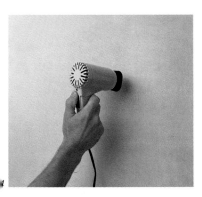

3 After about 1 to 1½ hours, during which time the paint will have entered the early stages of the drying process, start dabbing, at intervals, a little clear, water-based crackle varnish onto the A4 test card. As soon as you can do this without the varnish cissing the drying eggshell, use a fine-bristled brush to apply a coat of the varnish over the real surface.

Brush it out very lightly, both up and down and from side to side. But do not apply too much pressure, or you will drag off the underlying paint. However, you must work quite fast as the varnish will start to dry very quickly – once this happens you will be unable to lay it off without leaving brushmarks behind.

4 The surface should now be left to dry out. As it does so, fine cracks will begin to appear in the varnish. (At this stage you will need to look very closely at the surface to see them.) They are caused by the rapidly drying crackle varnish contracting and shrinking over the slower drying eggshell paint.

It is very difficult to pre-determine both the size and the pattern of cracks. However, by playing the hot air from a hairdryer over the surface they can be made slightly deeper and wider, and the whole crazing process speeded up.

5 When the surface is thoroughly dry, mix up a brown oil-based glaze (A), as shown left. (And see pages 87-8 on mixing glazes.) Rub this over the varnish and into the cracks, using a lint-free cotton rag.

6 Immediately, fold a clean piece of cotton rag into a flat-faced pad and wipe this over the surface to remove most of the glaze. And keep turning to a fresh face of the pad, so that you don't wipe colour back on again. By using a flat pad, the glaze remains in the cracks, thereby highlighting the intricate pattern of crazing across the surface.

When the surface has dried out, apply one or two coats of a matt or mid-sheen finish, clear oil-based varnish for protection (see page 89).

Note: You must never apply a water-based varnish on top of this finish, nor let it come into contact with water (or wet fingers!) before the oil-based varnish has been applied. In both instances the crackle varnish would begin to dissolve, thus ruining the effect.

VARIATIONS

All three crackle variations were created using the basic method in steps 1-4. However, in each case, a clear oil–, rather than water–, based varnish was applied in step 2. And in step 3, sepia and red inks were applied for **Variation A,** blue gouache was used for **Variation B,** and gray-green emulsion was employed for **Variation C.**

Two-colour distressing

A very adaptable technique, two-colour distressing is suitable for decorating walls anywhere around the home. And it is especially effective when taken over dado and picture rails, to blend them into the surround – this can make a room appear more spacious. The yellow-green/blue-green example illustrated here has been lightened and softened with a milky-white glaze. However, this is an optional adjustment to the final composition that can be omitted if a darker, stronger finish is required. This softening option has also been applied to the colour and pattern variations shown opposite, at the end of the step-by-step instructions.

GLAZES

If desired, the glazes specified below can be substituted for proprietary emulsions thinned 50/50 with water. Just match the colour swatches to the manufacturer's colour card.

A 40% white vinyl matt emulsion, 30% yellow-green acrylic, 25% ultramarine acrylic, and 5% black acrylic – then diluted 50/50 with water.

B 60% ultramarine acrylic, 25% permanent green acrylic, and 15% white vinyl matt emulsion – then diluted 50/50 with water.

C White vinyl matt emulsion diluted 50/50 with water.

1 Apply a minimum of two coats of a pale yellow eggshell paint over a previously prepared surface (see pages 74-6). Use either a smooth pile roller or a standard decorators' brush, and lightly rub down each coat after it has dried (approximately 24 hours) with wet and dry paper.

2 Soak a lint-free cotton rag in white spirit and wipe it over the ground coat – which should then be rubbed down immediately with a block of paraffin wax (available from artists' suppliers or hardware stores), to leave a thin film of wax on the surface (including any mouldings). The white spirit will break down the wax and thus help you to achieve a fairly even coverage.

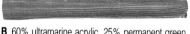

1

2

3

4

5

6

3 Mix up a yellow-green emulsion glaze (A), as shown left. (And see pages 87-8 on mixing glazes.) Then wipe it over the waxed surface with a smooth-faced decorators' sponge. Use a gentle scrubbing action, in all directions, to slowly build up subtle gradations of translucent colour over the ground coat.

4 If you wish to adjust the composition and break down a build-up of colour in some areas, gently rub the surface with a pad of cotton rag moistened with a little white spirit. This will remove both wax and glaze.

5 After the surface has been allowed to dry thoroughly, wax it again. Then mix up a blue-green glaze (B), as shown left. (And see pages 87-8 on mixing glazes.) And rub and wipe it over the surface with a smooth sponge, as in step 3. Once again the object is to build up cloudy blue patches of varying opacity, which allow the underlying yellow-green ground to ghost through. Then allow the surface to dry for 3 to 4 hours.

6 Moisten a kitchen scourer, or similar abrasive pad, with a little white spirit, and rub it quite firmly over the surface. Your purpose is to remove excess wax and any 'scrub marks' left by the sponge, and to break up patches of blue glaze where you might wish to see more of the underlying yellow-green ground – the latter being largely a matter of personal preference.

7 If you wish to soften and tone down the colours, dilute a white vinyl matt emulsion 50/50 with water to make a very translucent glaze (C), as shown left. Then gently wipe it over the surface with a smooth decorators' sponge. This process can be repeated if you think a further adjustment to the overall appearance of the finish is necessary.

Please note that in this example the thinned white glaze is wiped over the dado rail, thereby softening and blending it into the surrounding wall. However, by leaving the rail unsoftened it can be made into a

7

contrasting feature.

After the surface has dried thoroughly, a further option is to apply one coat of a matt or mid-sheen, clear oil-based varnish for protection (see page 89).

VARIATIONS

Variation A was created using two shades of beige coloured glaze over a white ground, and **Variation B** was achieved using two shades of blue over a pale yellow ground. Steps 1-8 were followed in both examples.

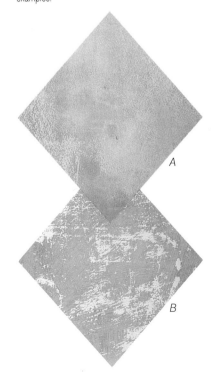

A

B

Aquarium

As the name suggests, this finish employs softened, translucent glazes to create a subtle aquatic effect that is particularly appropriate on flat surfaces in bathrooms (though it can work equally well elsewhere in the home). For the best results, only work on a couple of square yards or metres at a time (any adjacent sections can be blended in later on – see page 76), spend time softening the glazes to increase the illusion of depth in the finish, and give some thought to the sort of atmosphere you wish to create in the room, adjusting the tranquility of the compositon accordingly (see steps 5 to 9 below).

GLAZES

A 35ml French blue and 50ml white artists' oils per litre of 30% scumble, 20% linseed oil and 50% white spirit.

B 25ml ultramarine, 45ml white, 15ml black, 10ml French blue artists' oils per litre of 30% scumble, 20% linseed oil and 50% white spirit.

C Silver artists' oil – unthinned.

D 30ml cadmium red, 100ml white, and 5ml chrome yellow artists' oils per litre of 30% scumble, 30% linseed oil and 40% white spirit.

E As (D), but use 200ml white artists' oil.

1 Apply a minimum of two coats of pale blue eggshell paint over the previously prepared surface (see pages 74-6), to establish an unbroken expanse of opaque colour. Preferably use a smooth pile roller rather than a brush, and lightly rub down each coat after it has dried (approximately 24 hours) with wet and dry paper.

2 Mix up a light blue glaze (A) and a darker blue glaze (B) – as shown left. (And see pages 87-8 on mixing glazes.) Charge a textured sponge (see page 81) with glaze (A), removing any excess on a spare piece of paper, and gently dab it over the surface to create softly undulating, cloudy diagonal bands.

1

2

3

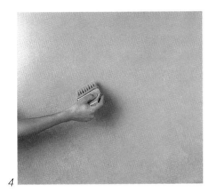

4

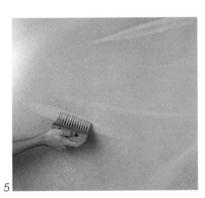

5

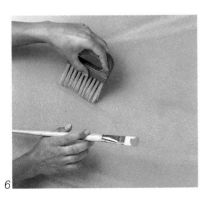

6

3 While glaze (A) is still wet, sponge on glaze (B) to fill in the gaps and cover the ground coat. Where they overlap, dab the glazes with the sponge to blend them together.

4 While both glazes are still wet, lightly dab a dry stippling brush over the surface to soften, blend and tone down the two colours. Regularly clean the brush on rag, to avoid any build-up of glaze. But leave some areas darker than others, to create the illusion of depth in the 'water'.

5 Again while the surface is still wet, dab and push the bristles of a dry edge stippler into the glaze to remove and re-distribute colour, and create large, elongated 'fish' shapes that 'float' at various angles across the surface. Keep cleaning the brush on a piece of rag, to avoid putting colour back on. Then allow the surface to dry for 24 hours.

When deciding on your composition, bear in mind that light, oval shapes impart a feeling of tranquility, while more elongated outlines create a greater sense of movement.

6 Use an artists' brush to apply the light blue glaze (A) in a series of shorter, thinner and slightly curved strokes that 'swim' at random through the 'water'. They should be irregularly spaced, but roughly follow a predominant diagonal (here, top left to bottom right).

Lightly dab each one with a small edge stippler, to soften and blend their outline into the background. But by leaving some darker than others you will add to the sense of 'depth' in the final composition.

7 Apply silver artists' oil (C), as shown left, with a small brush, to highlight the top edges of some of the larger, pale 'fish' and represent shafts of light glinting off their 'scales'.

8 Mix up a dark (D) and a light (E) coral pink glaze, as shown left. (And see pages 87-8 on mixing glazes.) Use two dry artists' brushes to dab on the glazes in short strokes, that appear to gently undulate and float in small 'shoals' through the 'water'. Don't overdo the use of these vibrant colours – as they

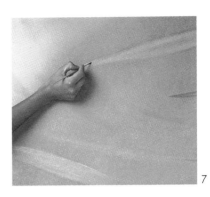

7

8

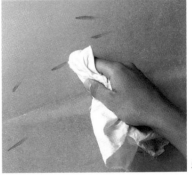

9

can dominate the final effect.

9 While they are still wet, lightly soften the tails of the small pink 'fish', using a clean, lint-free cotton rag. Again, this will help to create a sense of gentle movement through the 'water'.

Allow the surface to dry. Then apply two coats of a clear, matt finish water-based varnish for protection (see page 89).

Blazer

The dramatic finish illustrated here suggests a powerful conflagration of billowing smoke and heat. As such it is best confined to fairly small areas, like inset panelling, alcoves and flush doors. However, by substituting paler glazes (see opposite) the overall effect can be made lighter, less intense, and therefore more suitable for larger surfaces. On a long wall it is preferable if one person applies the glaze to a couple of square yards or metres at a time, while another follows with the softening brush. This will make it easier to blend adjacent sections together (see page 76).

GLAZE

A 40% black eggshell paint, 10% gold metallic oil paint, 10% linseed oil and 40% white spirit.

1 Apply a minimum of two coats of a fluorescent orange/red eggshell paint over the previously prepared surface (see pages 74-6), to establish an unbroken expanse of opaque colour. Use either a smooth pile roller or a standard decorators' brush, and rub down each coat after it has dried (approximately 24 hours) with wet and dry paper.

2 Mix up a translucent, black coloured glaze (A), containing a small quantity of gold metallic paint, as shown left. (And see pages 87-8 on mixing glazes.) Using a textured sponge (see page 81), dab the thin, runny glaze over the surface to form billowing, cloudy shapes through which the underlying orange/red ground shows through, at random, in small patches.

1

2

3

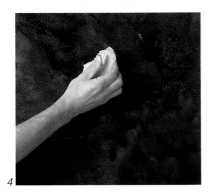

4

5

6

3 Use a badger softener to spread and soften out the still wet glaze. Work on an area of about a square foot (30 sq cms) at a time, and lightly sweep the brush over the surface in all directions. The object is to create a more cloudy and less stridently marked finish, through which the underlying ground coat ghosts through with varying degrees of intensity.

4 Allow the glaze to dry for about 10-20 minutes, and then gently dab on more of the black glaze (A) in random patches over the surface, again using a textured sponge. How much glaze you add depends on the finish you are trying to achieve. Broadly, the more black you sponge on, the darker, and therefore more intense and brooding, the effect.

5 While the glaze is still wet, soften it out with a badger brush, working on a patch of approximately a square foot (30 sq cms) at a time. Give each section its own distinct sense of movement by stroking the brush over the glaze in one direction only, in a series of short gentle sweeps within a 180 degree fan shape. Adjacent sections can then be 'fanned out' in different directions.

Remember to keep wiping the brush on a piece of rag, to avoid smearing glaze back over the surface.

6 A further option is to charge a fitch with white spirit, hold it some 5-6 ins (12-15 cms) from the surface, and run your finger through the bristle to send a fine spray over the still wet glaze. The droplets of spirit will 'ciss', or open up, small, circular patches of glaze, around which the black pigment will coalesce, and in the centre of which the orange/red ground coat will be more apparent. These patches should be softened and blended immediately with the badger brush.

N.B. Because this technique can be quite difficult to control, practice it first on a spare piece of paper pinned to a wall. And, if you find it necessary, add a little clear scumble to stop the white spirit running down the vertical surface.

Allow the finished composition to dry thoroughly, and then apply one coat of a matt, mid-sheen or gloss finish, clear oil-based varnish for protection (see page 89).

VARIATIONS

Variation A was created by applying a slower drying gray glaze over a blue eggshell ground. **Variation B** was achieved by applying just one pinky-brown glaze over an off-white eggshell ground. And **Variation C** was created using a gray and metallic silver glaze over a white eggshell ground. In each case the method shown in steps 1-7 was used.

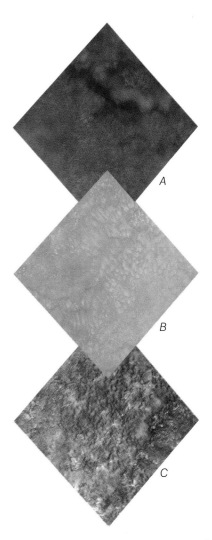

A

B

C

Tiffany

The iridescent Tiffany effect is a soft, subtle finish that can be used over large and small areas alike – though the former requires two people (refer to page 76 for advice on blending adjacent sections together). In the step-by-step illustrations below, four pastel-coloured glazes are used. However, any number of harmonious colours can be combined to good effect and made lighter or darker at various points along a surface to compensate for changes in the quality of the lighting – as in a long corridor. Impressive results will only be achieved by working on a smooth, unblemished ground coat.

GLAZES

A 60ml white, 10ml burnt Sienna and 3ml cadmium red artists' oils per litre of 30% scumble glaze, 20% linseed oil and 50% white spirit.

B 60ml white, 10ml Prussian blue and 3ml primrose yellow artists' oils per litre of medium as in (A) above.

C 60ml white and 10ml French blue artists' oils per litre of medium as in (A) and (B) above.

D 100ml white, 10ml black and 3ml raw umber per litre of medium as in (A), (B) and (C) above.

1 Apply a minimum of two coats of navy blue eggshell paint over the previously prepared surface (see pages 74-6), to establish an unbroken expanse of opaque colour. This subtle finish requires a very smooth ground coat, so preferably use a smooth pile roller, rather than a brush. And rub down each coat after it has dried (approximately 24 hours) with wet and dry paper.
2 Mix up four glazes: pink (A), green (B), blue (C), and gray (D), as shown left. (And see pages 87-8 on mixing glazes.) Dip a textured sponge (see page 81) into the pink glaze (A), remove any excess on a spare piece of lining paper, and dab the colour in random patches over the surface – softening them out by lightly dabbing with the sponge, as you go. And push the sponge firmly into any sections of moulding, to ensure a thorough distribution of the glaze.

1

2

3

4

5

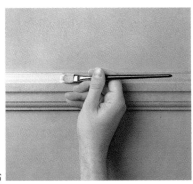

6

3 While the first colour is still wet apply the green glaze (B) with a clean sponge, using the same method as in step 2. Where any patches slightly overlap, blend and soften their edges together with the sponge. However, avoid superimposing one colour directly on top of another one – try to keep the colours distinct.

4 While the first and second colours are still wet, apply the blue (C) and gray (D) glazes one after the other, as in steps 2 and 3, until the ground coat is completely covered. Use a clean sponge for each glaze.

Again, soften and blend together the edges of patches that slightly overlap, but remember to avoid transferring colour from one patch to the centre of another.

5 While all the glazes are still wet, take a dry stippling brush and lightly dab it over the surface to tone down and soften the colours. Concentrate on one coloured patch at a time – starting from the centre and working outwards in a circular motion. Keep cleaning the brush on a rag, so that you remove glaze rather than put it back on elsewhere.

The more time and effort that you put into this stage – the more you work at breaking down any marked definition between one area of colour and another – the more subtle, and therefore effective, the final iridescent composition will be. However, you must work quite quickly, because once the glazes have dried further softening and blending is impossible.

6 A further option is to 'pick out' a section of any moulding that has been incorporated into the finish. The object is to provide a subtle contrast that helps to define the iridescent effect. To do this, use a small artists' brush to apply the pink glaze (A) along the curved top edge of the moulding.

7 Immediately, wipe off most of the glaze with a piece of cotton rag wrapped around your finger.

8 Then, dab a dry edge stippler over the glaze to tone down and soften the colour.

The surface should be allowed to

7

8

dry thoroughly before applying two coats of a matt or mid-sheen, clear water-based varnish for protection (see page 89).

VARIATION

This subtle Tiffany variation was created by applying pale pink, pale blue and pale green glazes over an off-white ground. The method shown in steps 1-5 was used.

Beast

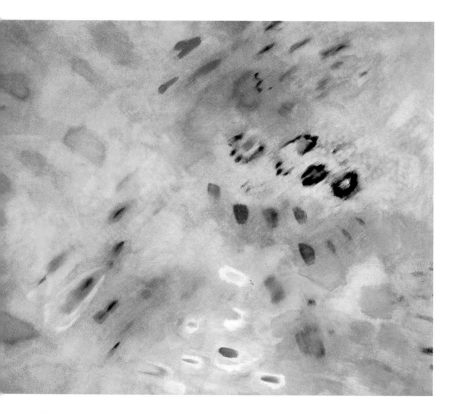

A dramatic, versatile finish, the beast effect looks equally good on fabric, such as curtains, blinds and cushion covers, as on walls and doors. The colours used for the mottled background and the prominent markings can be changed to suit the atmosphere you want to produce. For example, the addition of closely grouped, darker red and black spots will lend a more aggressive air to the finish, while softer, paler earth-coloured patches should strike a calmer, tamer note. (Refer to pages 90-3 for guidance on the use of colour.) Finally, large areas are better tackled by two people – see page 76.

GLAZES

A 30ml Oxford ochre and 10ml burnt umber artists' oils per litre of 70% gloss finish, clear oil-based varnish and 30% linseed oil.

B 40ml raw Sienna artists' oil per litre of medium as in (A) above.

C Burnt umber artists oil – unthinned.

D Burnt Sienna artists' oil – unthinned.

E Black artists' oil – unthinned.

F White artists' oil – unthinned.

1 Apply a minimum of two coats of off-white eggshell paint over the previously prepared surface (see pages 74-6), to establish an unbroken expanse of opaque colour. Use either a standard decorators' brush or a smooth pile roller, and rub down each coat after it has dried (approximately 24 hours) with wet and dry paper.
2 Mix up a light brown glaze (A), and a darker brown glaze (B), as shown left. (And see pages 87-8 on mixing glazes.) Apply both the glazes, striking the glider brush out in all directions, to form irregular-shaped, overlapping patches which cover the pale ground coat. At this stage the brushmarks should be seen to strike out in all directions.

1

2

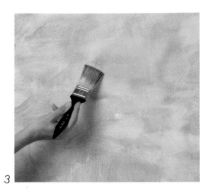

3

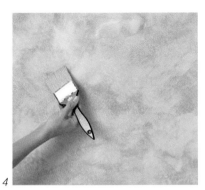

4

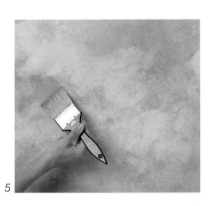

5

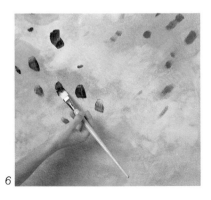

6

3 Mix up a clear medium consisting of 70 percent gloss finish, clear oil-based varnish and 30 percent linseed oil. Then use the glider to brush this out over the still wet surface to soften and blend the brown glazes into each other and get rid of the brushmarks, thereby creating subtle gradations of lighter and darker translucent colour over the ground.

4 While the surface is drying, drag a dry brush across some of the lighter patches and channels to wipe out the glaze and reveal more of the paler ground.

5 If it is felt necessary, the contrast between lighter and darker areas can be accentuated in places by brushing on and softening more of glazes (A) and (B). Then allow the surface to dry for 24 hours.

6 Squeeze small quantities of (C) burnt umber, (D) burnt Sienna, (E) black and (F) white artists' oils – as shown left – onto a palette, and then float a thin film of the clear medium used in step 3 over the surface, with a lint-free cotton rag.

Using a fitch or an artists' brush moistened with the clear medium, apply the burnt umber and burnt Sienna oils in a series of short dabs and strokes. The size, position and spacing of these small spots and patches is a matter of composition. But as a general rule, try to establish a number of identifiable groupings, each with its own directional accent, as in the illustrations.

7 Use a glider brush moistened with the clear medium to soften the spots, dragging the bristles over the surface to accentuate the direction of each group. Keep cleaning the brush, so that you don't transfer one colour to another. And leave some spots unsoftened, to provide a stronger contrast against the background.

8 Now apply and soften the black and white oils in the same manner – varying the size and opacity of the spots, and introducing markings such as the black 'paw prints'.

9 Introduce smaller spots, or 'eyes', of contrasting colour into the centre of some of the spots and

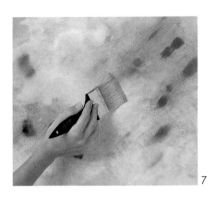

7

8

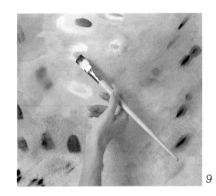

9

patches. As here, burnt umber on white, and black on red.

Allow the surface to dry thoroughly, and then apply one coat of a gloss finish, clear oil-based varnish to darken and enrich the colours, and for protection.

Nebula

The dramatic nebula finish shown here looks just as impressive over entire ceilings and walls as it does on smaller surface areas, such as wall panels, which can be presented as windows into 'space'. In both instances, give some thought to the composition of the finish before you begin to paint, and relate this to the type of ambiance you wish to create in a room. For example, the glazes can be adjusted to make them lighter or darker, warmer or colder, and the swirling sense of movement can be accentuated or diminished. Finally, over large areas, work on no more than a couple of square yards or metres at a time (see page 76).

GLAZES

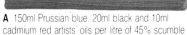

A 150ml Prussian blue, 20ml black and 10ml cadmium red artists' oils per litre of 45% scumble and 55% white spirit.

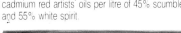

B 100ml ultramarine, 20ml black and 20ml cadmium red artists' oils per litre of medium as in (A) above.

C 60ml white eggshell and 10ml burnt Sienna artists' oils per litre of medium as in (A) above.

D 50% goldfinger plus 50% clear mid-sheen, oil-based varnish. This mix then thinned in a ratio of 70% glaze to 30% white spirit.

1 Apply a minimum of two coats of mid-blue eggshell paint over the previously prepared surface (see pages 74-6), to establish an unbroken expanse of opaque colour. Preferably use a smooth pile roller, rather than a standard decorators' brush, and rub down each coat after it has dried (approximately 24 hours) with wet and dry paper.

2 Mix up four glazes: (A) a dark blue, (B) a darker blue-black, (C) a pinky white, and (D) a gold colour, as shown left. (And see pages 87-8 on mixing glazes.) Use a textured sponge (see page 81) to dab the dark blue glaze (A) over the surface, in cloudy interlinked bands that allow the ground coat to show through in irregular shaped patches.

1

2

3

4

5

6

3 While the first glaze is still wet, sponge on the darker blue-black glaze (B) to cover the rest of the ground coat and, in places, overlap and blend into the first glaze. Use the sponge to soften some sections more than others. This will increase the sense of depth in the finish.

4 Again while the first two glazes are still wet, dab the pinky white glaze (C) onto the surface with a clean sponge. Try to create small clusters of broken, irregular-shaped patches, that are spaced at random. Where they are positioned is largely a matter of composition, but use the illustration for guidance.

5 While the pinky white patches are still wet, soften and drag them out with a dry badger brush. Work the bristles over the glaze in a series of short, curved sweeps to create a sense of swirling movement across the surface.

6 Charge an artists' brush or angled fitch with the gold glaze (D), hold it some 5-6 ins (12-15 cms) from the surface, and pull a finger through the bristles to spatter fine droplets of glaze at random over the composition.

N.B. Because this technique can be difficult to control, it is advisable to practice first on a spare piece of paper.

7 Use the badger brush to soften some of the gold flecks, especially those clustered around the white 'clouds'.

7a Note how the gold glaze has been softened out in one direction, especially in the top left hand corner, to accentuate the sense of swirling movement in the finish.

8 While the glazes are drying, stand back from the surface you are working on to assess the overall composition of the work. Now is the time to make any adjustments that you think are necessary. For example, the finish may need darkening or lightening in places. So, simply dab on the appropriate glaze with a sponge, gradually building up to the required level of capacity, and softening and blending the additional colour into the background as you go.

7

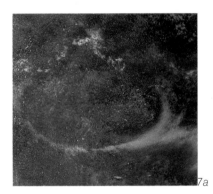

7a

8

Once you are satisfied with the finish, allow the surface to dry thoroughly, then apply one or two coats of a matt or mid-sheen, clear oil- or water-based varnish for protection (see page 89).

INDEX

USEFUL ADDRESSES

General supplies (paints, brushes, varnishes etc)

E. Ploton,
273 Archway Road,
London N6.

J.W. Bollom & Co,
314 Old Brompton Road,
London SW5.
&
15 Theobold's Road
London WC1.

Craig and Rose,
172 Leith Walk,
Edinburgh.

J.H. Ratcliffe and Co (Paints) Ltd.
135A Linaker Road,
Southport.

The Paint Service Co. Ltd,
19 Eccleston Street,
London SW1.

Lascaux artists' acrylics

Available from Alan Fitzpatrick,
16 Downs Court,
Amhurst Road,
London E8.

Fabric paints and dyes

Pebeo St-Marcel,
13367,
Marseille Cedex 11,
France.

Dylon International Ltd,
Worsley Bridge Road,
Lower Sydenham,
London SE26.

Durham Chemicals,
55–7 Glengall Road,
London SE15.

Solvex chemical-resistant gloves

Greenham Trading,
Telford Place,
Crawley,
West Sussex.

ACKNOWLEDGEMENTS

Picture Credits

Aqua Ware Ltd: 60–1, 62T
B.C. Sanitan: 63
Michael Boys Syndication: 29
Camera Press: 15, 50–1
Davies Keeling Trowbridge: 8, 9T, 14, 17, 18, 27TR, 28B, 44, 49, 51CR, 56BL, 56C,
68, 89
C.P. Hart: 60BL
Interior Space/Frances Denny: 75
John Lewis of Hungerford: 42–3, 56–7
Macdonald/Orbis: 6, 9B, 10, 11L, 11R, 16B, 20, 22–3, 28T, 30–1, 34, 36–7, 40–1, 43,
47R, 50BL, 52L, 54, 64, 66, 70, 76–7, 78–87, 90–1 (NB 16 paint finish Michael
Synder, interior design Augusta Kaye of Trio Design; 22–3, 30–1, 35–7 paint finish
Michael Synder, interior design Frances Gilles of IPL Interiors.)
Maison de Marie-Claire: /C. Pataut, Photo & M. Bayle, Stylist 38–9
/A. Maclean, Photo & Mahé, Stylist 46–7
/G. Bouchet, Photo & Orly, Stylist 48–9
NEXT Interiors: 24–5
Pipe Dreams: 62B
Fritz von der Schulenburg:/ Geoffrey Lamb, Paint Specialist &
Monika Apponyi, Designer 16T/CVP Design 19; 26–7, 39R/Paul & Janet Czainski,
Paint Specialists & David Mlinaric Designer 58–9
Smallbone of Devizes: 69
Syndication International: 12, /Options 32–3
Elizabeth Whiting Associates: /Michael Dunne 52–3; /Dek Messecar Design 67

Every effort has been made to trace the paint finish specialists and we apologise
in advance for any unintentional omissions. We would be pleased to insert the
appropriate acknowledgement in any subsequent edition of this publication.

Macdonald Orbis would like to thank Michael Synder, Trio Design Ltd of 2 St
Barnabas Street, London SW1 and IPL Interiors of 44 Fulham Rd, London SW3
for their help in finding locations, and Cherry of Cherry and Co. and
Wesley-Barrell for loaning furniture for photographs.